Teacher-Tested

Classroom Management

Strategies

Blossom S. Nissman, Ed.D.
Georgian Court College
Lakewood, NJ

Merrill,
an imprint of Prentice Hall
Upper Saddle River, New Jersey   *Columbus, Ohio*

Editor: Debra A. Stollenwerk
Production Editor: JoEllen Gohr
Cover Designer: Diane C. Lorenzo
Covert Art: © Photodisk, Inc.
Production Manager: Pamela Bennett
Director of Marketing: Kevin Flanagan
Marketing Manager: Suzanne Stanton
Marketing Coordinator: Krista Groshong

Printed in the United States of America

10 9 8 7

ISBN: 0-13-022254-2

INTRODUCTION

This booklet was developed in response to pre-school to high school level teachers' concerns regarding the management of their classrooms and productive relationships with administration, their colleagues, and parents and within their communities.

The concerns were then given to their peers who have demonstrated success in the classroom responding to management problems. Each of the five teachers provided his/her professional responses, which are presented in this booklet. All the processes and procedures have been used effectively by these master teachers.

In addition, a successful and original classroom management program is presented providing the reader with guidelines for implementing this program. Any reader interested in more detailed information concerning the "Ticket to Classroom Management Success" program should contact Ann Weinbrenner (609-597-3535) or Dr. Blossom Nissman (609-978-0876).

This booklet is designed to assist and encourage innovation in teaching and to present management methods that will give the classroom teacher the freedom to provide each child with maximum opportunities to learn. Those of us who worked diligently on this project sincerely hope that our efforts will enhance the instructional quality of the classrooms of those who use the ideas and suggestions presented.

The editor would also like to acknowledge the work of Dr. Martin L. Stamm, who was involved in the original project and contributed a great deal to the professional quality of this publication.

Blossom S. Nissman, Ed.D.
Professor of Education
Georgian Court College
Lakewood, NJ 08071

SPECIAL NOTE

In order to provide a variety of approaches, the editor has included a few statements with which she cannot fully agree. These are presented to provide the reader with an opportunity for selective choice among the options presented. Keeping in mind that the welfare of the student is the teacher's primary concern, these techniques can be effective in the classrom if used with moderation as an integral part of the classroom climate for productive learning.

Teachers Contribution

Candice Bradley
Mary Ann Klicka
John Misieczko
Carrie Rudolph
Steven Rosenbloom
Ann Weinbrenner

DEDICATION:

To Christopher and Danielle Nissman

and

Kelsey and Kendall Young

my grandchildren

Whose bright and creative minds, love of learning, and enthusiasm

for the joys of each day provide me with confidence and hope as they

prepare to build a safe and productive world of tomorrow

In memory of

Dr. Martin L. Stamm

1917 – 1991

Scholar

Visionary

Colleague

Mentor

Friend

TABLE OF CONTENTS

D

F

H

I

xi

MANAGEMENT PROBLEM:	*ABSENTEEISM*

TEACHER'S CONCERN:

What can teachers do in order to deal more effectively with students who are absent excessively for any number of reasons (e.g., illnesses, family responsibilities and school phobias)?

WORKABLE OPTIONS:

1. Reinforce students whenever they attend school with a special activity and/or event of their own choosing (e.g., ten minutes of talking with classmates).

2. Provide individual conferences for those students who are fearful of school (e.g., anxiety about failure).

3. Have the student role play the feared situation in the presence of the teacher. After rehearsing alternative ways of responding to the fear of the student, try several actual everyday situations.

4. Contact parents to find out why the student isn't regularly attending school. (In some cases, duties at home have a higher priority than school attendance.)

5. Place the student who is frequently absent in a group with two other students whom he/she is friends with, but who come to school regularly. Tell him/her that his/her regular attendance will earn points for the group. At the end of the week, those points can be exchanged for a special activity of the group's choosing.

6. Send home class and/or homework assignments via friends, relatives, and personal phone calls so that the student doesn't fall behind the rest of the class.

7. Individualize instruction for those students who have returned to school from a long period of absence, so that they will not fall behind the rest of the class.

8. Refer the student who is continually absent to the appropriate supportive school personnel (counselor, attendance officer, nurse, etc.).

MANAGEMENT PROBLEM:	*ADJUSTING TO SCHOOL ROUTINES*
TEACHER'S CONCERN:	How do you help students adjust to the routine of the school day?
WORKABLE OPTIONS:	

1. While sitting in a circle with students, ask them to share their ideas of favorite activities in school. This information can be used to set up the routine.

2. On a monthly basis, while sitting in a circle with students, ask them to share their feelings about their daily routine. If necessary, make changes.

3. Post the daily routine of the classroom on a bulletin board.

4. Establish a game called "a rabbit" or "a turtle". Students who follow the daily routine and get their work done receive a paper rabbit on their desks. Those who have trouble adjusting to the routine receive a turtle and encouragement to work for a rabbit.

5. On a weekly basis, evaluate the students and discuss with them their adjustment to the school routine.

6. For younger students, provide a break (such as a fruit break) between morning academic sessions.

2

MANAGEMENT PROBLEM:	*AFTER-SCHOOL JOB INTEREST RESULTS IN ACADEMIC PROBLEMS*
TEACHER'S CONCERN:	A student's academic performance is dropping as a result of his/her after-school job. How can teachers help students maintain an acceptable level of achievement?
WORKABLE OPTIONS:	

1. Ask the student's parents to limit the number of hours that he/she can work (e.g., reduce a seven-hour day to three hours). Source: Cole, S. "Send Our Children to Work." Psychology Today, July 1997, 14 (2), p. 68.

2. Recommend to the student's parents that he/she be allowed to work only on weekends.

3. If the student is failing several courses, encourage him/her to take a leave of absence from work until his/her grades are acceptable.

4. Talk to the student's employer about the problem, and request that he/she urge the student to keep up with his/her school work.

5. Provide individual conferences for the student to discuss his/her academic responsibilities. Discuss the student's priorities and actual need for earnings.

6. Suggest an in-school cooperative education program to the student and parents. (The student may need more structure and support.)

7. Propose a vocational school to the student and parents.

8. Refer the student to the school guidance counselor.

9. Use parental and/or administrative pressure on the student when all other options have been exhausted.

MANAGEMENT PROBLEM:	*ALCOHOL USE*

TEACHER'S CONCERN:

A student comes to class inebriated. What should the teacher do?

WORKABLE OPTIONS:

1. Immediately send the student to the principal's office and have him/her detained until you can talk to him/her.

2. Notify parents of the student's condition.

3. Ask the school psychologist and/or guidance counselor to talk to the student.

4. Seek administrative support in this matter. Refer to your teacher's manual for the procedure to be followed.

5. Follow up on referrals on a daily basis.

6. If the student has been suspended from school, contact the parents and inquire about the student.

7. Remind students periodically about the school's policy regarding drinking.

8. Provide private follow-up conferences with the student to discuss his/her reasons for drinking.

4

MANAGEMENT PROBLEM:	*ANNOYING CLASSROOM DISTRACTIONS*

TEACHER'S CONCERN:	How can a teacher prevent irritating classroom behaviors?

WORKABLE OPTIONS:

1. Have the students and teacher first discuss and then write a "group" contract adopting acceptable classroom rules and procedures by the end of the first week of school.

2. Periodically review the rules and procedures of the classroom until the students can successfully adhere to them.

3. Use simple verbal reprimands when the misbehavior occurs. Make sure that they are to the point, moderate in tone, and private (e.g., "Stop talking and work on your math problems, please.").

4. Give praise to the entire class as frequently as possible (e.g., "Thank you for working so quietly" or "I'm delighted to see you all working so well today.") .

5. A student who continually exhibits an unacceptable behavior (e.g., out of seat) might profit from an "individualized" contract pinpointing the "desired" behavior (e.g., remaining in his/her seat) and delineating the consequences (e.g., if goal is reached, then student will receive designated reward or recognition).

6. Intervene as soon as possible in order to prevent the misbehavior from occurring (e.g., "Harry, may I help you with your assignment?" as the student begins to show signs of frustration) .

7. Use facial expressions to convey to the student that the misbehavior was not totally overlooked. Circulate around the room frequently, to avert potential behavior problems.

MANAGEMENT PROBLEM:	*ANTAGONISM WITH AUTHORITY*
TEACHER'S CONCERN:	What can be done to help students improve their interaction with authority figures?
WORKABLE OPTIONS:	

1. Provide opportunities for students to change their hostile and aggressive energy into socially acceptable channels such as sports, clubs, crafts, hobbies, etc.

2. Give students reading and/or writing assignments that deal with antagonistic behaviors and ask them to comment on different socially acceptable ways of handling conflict situations.

3. Praise the students whenever they are cooperating with other adults (e.g., "That was very kind of you to help her find her keys") .

4. Talk to the student in private to ascertain the reason for his/her misbehavior.

5. Provide the students with models of appropriate communicative behavior through role playing activities.

6. Encourage students to strive for greater self-control in as many situations as possible.

7. Emphasize to the students the difference that exists between acceptable communication in school and those that are used at home and/or in the community.

8. Contact parents and/or administrators when there is no other way of resolving the conflict situation.

9. Refer the student to the appropriate members of the Child Study Team if the student frequently displays uncontrollable verbal hostility. Keep anecdotal records to support your concerns.

MANAGEMENT PROBLEM:	*ARGUMENTATIVE STUDENT*
TEACHER'S CONCERN:	How can the teacher deal with a child who becomes argumentative upon confrontation?
WORKABLE OPTIONS:	1. Do not confront the student in a group situation.

1. Do not confront the student in a group situation.

2. Do not use an accusatory tone upon approaching the student.

3. Evaluate the situation which led to the confrontation.

4. Do not back the student into a corner. Leave room for options.

5. Do not make threats which cannot be carried out.

6. Allow your emotions to cool before approaching the student.

7. Maintain an appearance of control at all times. Use a clear, firm voice.

8. Allow the child to have the opportunity to speak his/her piece.

9. Allow for role playing doing role reversal.

10. Try to explore and discover what led to the confrontation and avoid repeating these circumstances.

11. If you made an error, admit it!

MANAGEMENT PROBLEM:	*ATTENDANCE*

TEACHER'S CONCERN:

How can I get students to have better attendance in the classes I teach?

WORKABLE OPTIONS:

1. Get in touch with the family and discuss the problem.

2. Provide the student with activities that are open-ended and need follow up so he/she feels a responsibility to come to school the next day.

3. Make instruction meaningful to the student.

4. Reward the student if absenteeism decreases.

5. Discuss with the child the reason why he/she is absent.

6. Give the student responsibility in the classroom that demands daily attention. Help him/her understand that his/her absence will handicap group progress.

See section on *Absenteeism* for more suggestions.

MANAGEMENT PROBLEM:	*ATTENTION-GETTING BEHAVIOR*
TEACHER'S CONCERN:	What do I do about student who exhibit attention-getting behavior?
WORKABLE OPTIONS:	

1. Examine the cause of the behavior. Is it due to poor self-concept or being ignored, or is there a potential learning disability? Follow up on what you discover with appropriate school personnel.

2. Examine your reaction to the behavior and then change it if your behavior triggers a negative response.

3. Role play. Give students a situation and have them play out acceptable and unacceptable behavior.

4. Discuss with the student in private the behavior that is not appropriate.

5. Ignore the behavior, if possible, so it cannot be used as attention-getting.

6. Set up class rules in the beginning of the year and be consistent in enforcing them (Cantor's Assertive Discipline program, for example) .

7. Use various modalities when giving directions. Write as well as say the assignment so all understand. Give examples and check the student's progress by moving around the room.

8. Examine your task assignments. Are they too difficult for some students? Are they clear? Be flexible. Change. Modify when necessary.

9. Give an abundance of praise. Student will strive for positive reinforcement from the teacher.

10. Attach consequences to the undesirable attention-getting behavior. Keep an accurate record of when each occurs for objective evaluation.

9

MANAGEMENT PROBLEM:	*ATTENTION-SEEKING WELL-BEHAVED STUDENT*
TEACHER'S CONCERN:	What can a teacher do with a child who is constantly seeking his/her attention?
WORKABLE OPTIONS:	

1. Explain to the child that he/she is an important person, but that other individuals and/or the entire class also need your attention. Continue to give individual attention to this child whenever feasible, but slowly reduce it until it is equal to the amount you normally spend with a student.

2. Because there may be problems of which you may not be aware, the child should receive the services of the Child Study Team and the school counselor. The child will then get additional individual attention that may solve a problem that he/she is having.

3. If the child is from a single-parent family, you can, with the appropriate permission, recommend a "Big Brother or Sister" affiliation.

4. The attention-seeking child is many times a loner in the classroom. Carefully select another student to be his/her classroom "buddy." They are to do their assignments together as much as possible. This may fulfill the needs of the child and give the teacher more time for the other children. An appropriate "buddy" can be determined through a class sociogram.

5. Inform the parent(s) of the child's problem. Hopefully the parents will give the child more attention at home and alert you of any concerns that may relate to his/her need to seek attention in school.

MANAGEMENT PROBLEM:	*ATTITUDE CHANGE*

TEACHER'S CONCERN:

Some students have a bad attitude. No matter what you do, they cannot be motivated. How do I get them to change?

WORKABLE OPTIONS:

1. Ignore his/her attitude, but do not ignore his/her behavior. Do not let the student's negative attitude bother you. Talk personally with the student of your concerns.

2. Examine and change, if possible, the environment of the classroom. Make it brighter and cheerier. Use the interest of the students in decorating the room with their quality work and ideas.

3. Examine and adjust your teaching style. Are you too tense, sober, callous, demanding, sarcastic? Try to be more pleasant and excited about what you are teaching . Add humor and personalize your interaction with your students.

4. Plan your day so that "fun" things (activities that require movement and communication) occur between "work" periods.

5. Strive to present more chances for successful experiences to the student with the bad attitude. Give him/her earned and honest praise and encouragement at every opportunity.

6. Discuss with the class their plans for the future. Incorporate their career interests in your lessons. If students see the connection between what they are learning now and their future, they are more apt to be self-motivated.

7. Discuss with the class the importance of a positive attitude. Present situations and have members of the class role play characters with and without good attitudes in varying real-life situations.

MANAGEMENT PROBLEM:	*BATHROOM SHARING*

TEACHER'S CONCERN:

How can one bathroom be shared when there are a large number of students in the classroom?

WORKABLE OPTIONS:

CLASSROOM BATHROOMS

1. Discuss with your students the necessity for sharing the bathroom.

2. Set up a bathroom schedule.

3. Prior to lunch, when the use of the bathroom is more frequent, allow students to use the bathroom upon completion of assignments.

4. Set specific time limits on stay in the bathroom.

5. Refer any constant user to the school nurse in the event that a medical problem exists.

6. Use a rotating sign on the bathroom door to indicate whether the bathroom is occupied or unoccupied.

7. Never use the forbidden use of the bathroom as punishment.

HALL BATHROOMS

1. Clearly define bathroom rules from the first day of class.

2. Stress courtesy.

3. See rules above.

4. Provide a bathroom pass or sign out sheet with time noted so extended time (and mischief) in the bathroom is avoided.

MANAGEMENT	
PROBLEM:	*BEHAVIOR PROBLEMS*

TEACHER
CONCERN: What would be a simple but good discipline technique to use to resolve a child's's constant misbehavior?

WORKABLE
OPTIONS:
the

When a child exhibits unacceptable behavior, follow steps listed below:

1. If possible, meet with the child and describe in exact terms the behavior you find unacceptable in the classroom.

2. During the discussion, explain the reason(s) that you find the behavior unacceptable.

3. Be sure the child understands that it is not he or she who is unacceptable but rather the behavior.

4. Let the student know exactly what will happen if the problem continues.

5. If the misbehavior occurs again, follow through with the previously planned disciplinary action.

6. Throughout the process, keep the parents and the principal informed of the progress or lack of progress.

7. If the child continues to misbehave and you feel that you have utilized all of your options and resources, send the child to the principal's office. Explain to the child that he/she is welcome to return when he/she is ready to follow the classroom rules.

| MANAGEMENT PROBLEM: | *BOASTFUL, ATTENTION-SEEKING STUDENT* |

TEACHER'S CONCERN: What can be done for students who are constantly disrupting the class in order to gain the teacher's attention? (See *Attention-Getting Behavior and Attention-Seeking, Well-Behaved Student*)

WORKABLE OPTIONS:

1. Give the student a position of responsibility in the classroom and encourage him/her to set a good example for others (e.g., passing out papers) .

2. Post a chart in the front of the room delineating the rules to be followed when responding (e.g., (1) Raise your hand if you wish to talk; (2) Wait to be called on; (3) Listen while others talk, etc.) .

3. Assign the student a special project of interest and let him/her present the report to the class.

4. Ignore the student's annoying comments, but praise him/her when he/she tells of his/her real achievements.

5. Assign the student to a small group in which he/she must primarily participate as a follower.

6. Provide frequent recognition and positive attention whenever possible.

7. Model appropriate behavior every day for the student so that he/she can see what is expected of him/her (e.g., role playing by teacher and/or peers) .

8. Arrange parent conferences to discuss any factors that may be contributing to the student's problem in school (e.g., sibling rivalry) .

MANAGEMENT
PROBLEM: *BULLETIN BOARDS*

TEACHER'S
CONCERN: How can changing bulletin boards be made less time consuming?

WORKABLE
OPTIONS:
1. Maintain one bulletin board throughout the year for school menus, bulletins, calendars, and honor lists. Little change is needed in such an arrangement.

2. Designate one bulletin board for student work only. Appoint student helpers to post student work worthy of display.

3. Incorporate the making of a bulletin board scene as part of a lesson. Many learning skills are involved in such an activity.

4. Designate one bulletin board in the classroom for which the students are responsible. Appoint teams to design and change the scenes and displays when necessary.

5. Use the bulletin board for an exchange of information. Make an "I Want to Know" board. Students write questions down for which they would like the answers. Other students in the class are responsible for researching and supplying the answers.

6. See extensive suggestions on this topic in <u>New Dimensions in Elementary Guidance</u> by Martin L. Stamm and Blossom S. Nissman (New York: Richards Rosen Press, 1971).

MANAGEMENT PROBLEM:	*CALLING OUT IN CLASS - RESPONSE #1*
TEACHER'S CONCERN:	What do you do with a student who calls out answers or comments during class?
WORKABLE OPTIONS:	

1. Discuss your expectations with the class. Make up rules and consequences at the very beginning of the school year.

2. Keep a frequency record in your grade book of the calling out and increase the severity of the consequence in direct proportion to the frequency of the "calling out."

3. With children in the middle grades and older, divide the class into two groups and make a game out of questions and answers. Each team scores a point for each correct answer. If a team member calls out an answer out of turn, that team loses a set amount of points.

4. Praise the student who does not call out but waits to be called on.

5. Ignore the calling out. Do not acknowledge having heard it.

6. Use a strict behavior modification program to lessen and ultimately extinguish this behavior.

7. Examine the reason for calling out. Is it for attention? Do you overlook calling on this student? Is it a result of inability to sit still? Does this child have a learning disability? React to these symptoms appropriately.

8. Contact the parents. Try an at-home reward system for good days (days in which calling out did not occur). This will involve sending a daily note home.

MANAGEMENT
PROBLEM: *CALLING OUT IN CLASS - RESPONSE # 2*

TEACHER'S
CONCERN: I am extremely frustrated by children constantly
                            calling out in class even when the class is supposed to
                            be working quietly at their seats. What can I do
                            about it?

WORKABLE
OPTIONS: 1. Be sure that the students are aware of what you
                            expect of them concerning this problem. Instead of
                            calling out in class, explain what procedure you
                            want them to use and the reasoning for it if they
                            want your attention.

                            2. If students calling out is the major problem, have a
                            class meeting. Have the children make
                            recommendations to solve this problem. This
                            would include the type of discipline to be used for
                            the children who continue disturbing the class by
                            calling out.

                            3. Be consistent and persistent in disciplining the
                            children who call out.

                            4. If a child communicates with you by calling out,
                            make your only reaction one of displeasure and do
                            not answer the question or fulfill the request.

                            5. Tell the class that if calling out in class only occurs
                            a certain amount of times during the week, you will
                            do something special with them on Friday
                            afternoon. Peer pressure is then utilized in solving
                            the problem. Every new week the number of times
                            calling out in class is lowered, in order to receive the
                            special Friday activity.

                            6. Calling out may be motivated by enthusiasm or the
                            fear that he/she will forget what he/she wanted to
                            say. Have students keep a pad and pencil on their
                            desk to write down a thought they might forget so
                            they can refer to it when they finally get called
                            upon. Be sure to give everyone a chance to answer
                            something — even the slower thinking students!

17

MANAGEMENT PROBLEM:	*CHILDREN FROM BROKEN HOMES*
TEACHER'S CONCERN:	What can I do to aid the student during the separation and/or divorce of his/her parents?
WORKABLE OPTIONS:	1. If the student shows no signs of being affected by this experience, respect his/her privacy and do not bring the issue to his/her attention.

1. If the student shows no signs of being affected by this experience, respect his/her privacy and do not bring the issue to his/her attention.

2. If the student wants to talk. be an attentive listener but do not pry, take sides, or discuss information you have heard or learned from others.

3. Do not rationalize the child's changed behavior as understandable because his/her parents are having problems. Be sure that is the reason and then handle accordingly using the guidance and Child Study Team services available in your school.

4. Consider contacting one or both parents if there is significant change in the student's academic, social, or emotional behavior.

5. Perhaps you can have a small group session with several children in your class who have already been part of this experience within their home.

6. Often children feel a sense of responsibility when a separation takes place or there is much disruption at home. Give this student balance and an improved sense of self-worth by giving him/her responsibility in the classroom that requires his/her leadership.

7. Do not play "marriage counselor." Be non-committal in regard to the pros and cons regarding divorce. Be supportive of whatever living arrangements are made and if the child is to remain in your class, show your pleasure. If he/she is moved to another location and will be leaving you, encourage this move with positive support.

MANAGEMENT PROBLEM:	*CLASS CLOWN*

TEACHER'S CONCERN: How does one deal effectively with a "class clown"?

WORKABLE OPTIONS:

1. Let the student know in private how you feel about his/her unacceptable behavior and what is expected of him/her. Try to form a trusting relationship with this student. Listen to his/her feelings and expectations. Try to channel his/her talent for humor in a more productive vein, such as a class play or dramatic skit.

2. If you think it would be beneficial, do role playing with this student. Give him/her the role of the teacher with a specific objective to teach during a lesson. You take the role of the class clown and exhibit the same behaviors that he/she does in class. This may be a learning experience for the entire class!

3. Explain to the student that the solution to his/her problem is both his/her and your responsibility. However, if the "class clown" behavior continues and it affects the level of learning for the rest of the class, then the responsibility for the solution will lie with him/her and the administration.

4. Try to find the curriculum areas in which the student is interested. Give him/her some independent work in this area and observe any change in behavior.

5. Let the child gain the attention of the class in such a way that it has a positive affect on the class. The student could conduct mini lessons, lead study groups, assist students, or make other contributions that will benefit the entire class.

6. Ask the assistance of a counselor to investigate various possible reasons for the child's need to be the "class clown."

MANAGEMENT	
PROBLEM:	*CLASSROOM RULES*

TEACHER'S
CONCERN: What do you do when clear rules are set up in September, yet constant repetition of these rules is necessary for the student to follow them?

WORKABLE
OPTIONS:

1. In establishing class rules, make the list as short as possible. It is simple arithmetic to conclude that the fewer the rules you must enforce, the fewer disciplinary actions you have to take.

2. Make the class rules relevant by ensuring that all the class rules are firmly based on educational considerations.

3. Make the rules meaningful and share the logical relationship to the educational tasks at hand.

4. Make the list positive. A positive statement offers a goal to work toward rather than a veiled threat to avoid.

5. Establish the consequences if a rule is broken.

6. List the classroom rules in a prominent position on a bulletin board or the black board.

7. Reinforce positive responses to rules such as a student following a class rule by raising his/her hand instead of calling out an answer. Reinforce this with the positive response of "Thank you, John, for raising your hand to answer that question!"

8. Make a copy of the rules and distribute to all the students.

9. On a weekly basis, have a short conference with each student. Relate how they have followed the rules throughout the week and agree on successes, needs for change, and ideas for improvement in class routine.

MANAGEMENT PROBLEM:	*CLEANING UP WORK AREAS*

TEACHER'S CONCERN:

How can children be taught to clean work areas when they have finished using the area?

WORKABLE OPTIONS:

1. Establish clean-up rules at the beginning of the year.

2. Show the students where things belong.

3. Establish class guidelines on classroom order.

4. Have them practice "cleaning up."

5. Allow younger students more practice time than older ones.

6. Be consistent. Insist on "cleaning up" each time.

7. Provide adequate time for "clean up." Plan for it.

8. Emphasize neatness and cleanliness whenever possible during the day.

9. Praise those students who are neat and/or begin to clean up first.

10. Do not allow students who do not remember to clean up to use work areas for a period of time.

11. Use a bell or some other signal to signify clean-up time. As soon as students hear or see this signal, they are to begin cleaning up.

12. Make a "Success Day" chart . List clean-up as one success to be accomplished. Mark charts at the end of each day.

13. Make a check list of clean-up tasks. Attach to each work area.

14. Appoint student helpers to monitor peers.

MANAGEMENT PROBLEM:	*CLERICAL WORK*

TEACHER'S CONCERN: How can clerical duties be incorporated into the daily management of the classroom (lunch money collection, attendance, paper filing, etc.) ?

WORKABLE OPTIONS:

1. Appoint student helpers to collect money and to fill out daily forms.

2. Copy a list of your students' names. Leave room for several boxes next to each name. Use these forms to expedite collecting or counting procedures. Example :

Name	Lunch	Attendance	Homework
John	no	yes	yes

3. To help make the collection of money easier and more accurate, assign each child an envelope with his/her name on it. Children put money into these envelopes and close. Have student helper collect envelopes and place them in a small box.

4. To expedite the filing of papers, enlist your class as helpers. A variety of learning skills are involved in this procedure.

5. Be consistent in following a routine so the students feel comfortable with responding to your direction and are prepared to follow through on the materials you wish to collect, account for, etc.

6. Use a desk calendar to keep a record of what is due and when it is due so that you submit all reports and materials on time.

7. Check your teacher's manual carefully to determine how you order supplies, when you're responsible for bus duty, and what you are supposed to do and when you are to do it.

MANAGEMENT PROBLEM:	*COMMUNICATION WITH THE ADMINISTRATION*

TEACHER'S CONCERN:

Our building principal does not make himself available to assist in the daily problems that we confront as classroom teachers. What can we do about this?

WORKABLE OPTIONS:

1. Ask for a conference with the principal to honestly share your needs and see if it brings about a change.

2. If you feel uncomfortable about approaching the principal directly, send a note asking for his/her assistance in a particular situation and wait for a response. If there is no response, try the following procedures.

3. To solve certain types of problems, you may want to turn to individuals on the faculty who have taken on various leadership roles and whose professionalism you respect.

4. Many types of problems that face teachers daily can be alleviated by a person on staff often overlooked... the custodian. This person can be a tremendous resource, so develop a positive and functional relationship with him/her.

5. A liaison meeting between the teachers and administration may provide the opportunity to discuss such a problem.

6. As a new teacher, you have the "ear" and input from your mentor teacher. Be sure to take advantage of this source of information.

MANAGEMENT PROBLEM:	*CONTROLLING CLASSROOM STUDENTS WHILE INSTRUCTING INDIVIDUALS OR SMALL GROUPS*

TEACHER'S CONCERN:

What techniques can I use to control students at their seats while I am providing individual or small group instruction?

WORKABLE OPTIONS:

1. Have various enrichment activities readied for students when they are finished with their assigned work. Make the selection of the enrichment activities part of your daily lesson planning.

2. Be sure that the students understand what behavior is expected of them during their independent work. Place these "rules" on a poster and place it in view of the class. If any rule needs to be discussed, it can easily be pointed to on the poster and presented to the class.

3. If there are a few students who continually disrupt the class while working independently, place them in isolated locations in the classroom. Explain to them that they can have their previous seats when they are ready to follow the classroom rules during independent work time.

4. Select competent students who you feel are capable of being resource persons within the classroom. When you are working with a group, these resource students can assist the rest of the class in answering basic questions and supplying needed materials during their independent work time.

5. Ask the principal if he/she can schedule you to observe a teacher on the staff who effectively deals with this particular classroom management problem.

MANAGEMENT PROBLEM:	*COPING WITH THE DEATH OF A RELATIVE, PEER, OR FRIEND*
TEACHER'S CONCERN:	What can I do to aid a student who has lost a family member, a friend, or a fellow student?
WORKABLE OPTIONS:	1. Offer an open line of communication to the student by making him/her aware that you know of this sad event and would be willing to talk about it if he/she chooses.

1. Offer an open line of communication to the student by making him/her aware that you know of this sad event and would be willing to talk about it if he/she chooses.

2. Respond to the student's questions with honest and direct answers.

3. Keep in mind the child's age and his/her capacity to understand the enormity of the situation.

4. If a parent has died, try to communicate with the surviving parent and offer support in helping the child cope with the loss.

5. If a sibling or friend has died, a group discussion would be a reasonable approach. Through this discussion, students have the support of their peers and become quickly aware of the fact that they have common fears and concerns. The teacher leading this discussion must clearly avoid religious views and maudlin attitudes. A sense of concern and caring should permeate the discussion.

6. Allow time for the student to get back into the routine of school. Involve the school counselor and any other services available in the school if you think the child seems depressed or confused.

7. Recommend to the parent(s) a free copy of <u>Caring About Kids</u>: <u>Talking to Children About Death,</u> available from Public Inquiries, National Institute of Mental Health, 5600 Fishers Lane, Rockville, MD 20857.

MANAGEMENT PROBLEM:	*CURSING*
TEACHER'S CONCERN:	What do you do when a student curses at a teacher?
WORKABLE OPTIONS:	

1. Ignore it if it will become a central point in the classroom. Then try to work with the child in isolation concerning the offense.

2. Examine the causes of such language. Is it anger or habit? If it's in anger, work on teaching the student socially acceptable forms of expressing anger.

3. Role play or discuss socially acceptable ways of showing anger.

4. Initiate a behavior modification program to change habitual cursing.

5. Attach a consequence. Make sure the severity of the consequence is in direct proportion to the frequency of the cursing. Keep an accurate record, preferably in the back of the pupil's record book, of when the infraction happens.

6. Discuss the advantages of proper language. Provide word games in class, introducing new and sophisticated vocabulary to spark interest in alternate verbal expression.

7. Contact the parents. Get an idea of how they feel about this and enlist their support. Help them establish a reward system for days in which the frequency of cursing is diminished and subsequently eliminated.

8. Clearly make the point that cursing is not acceptable in school.

9. Refer the student to the school disciplinarian according to your Board policy or rules in the Teachers' Manual if this behavior persists.

MANAGEMENT PROBLEM:	*DAYDREAMING*
TEACHER'S CONCERN:	How can I help a child who is constantly daydreaming?
WORKABLE OPTIONS:	

1. If the student frequently exhibits this type of behavior, he/she should be referred to the Child Study Team to investigate possible causes. There may be a serious medical problem involved.

2. When you notice the child daydreaming, check later to see if the cause was a lack of understanding of the topic being discussed during the lesson. If this is the case, then the problem is not daydreaming but instead the child's lack of readiness in that particular subject area.

3. Make it a habit to ask the students questions during the teaching lesson. It will raise their attention level to know that at any time they must provide answers on the content of the lesson.

4. If you notice several students daydreaming, then try to develop lessons in which the students are more involved with the learning experience.

5. Make daily involvement in the classroom activities part of each student's evaluation. Try to give the students weekly feedback that reflects their improvement in this area.

6. Change the child's seat so looking out the window is not as inviting . Place him/her in the center of the classroom so he/she will feel like an integral member of the class .

MANAGEMENT PROBLEM:	*DEMANDING STUDENTS*

TEACHER'S CONCERN: How do you cope with a child who demands your constant attention?

WORKABLE OPTIONS:

1. Give this child a special job to show you care and have confidence in him/her.

2. Make this child captain or leader whenever possible.

3. Play games that nourish self-confidence. Circle game: Children try to name someone in circle who has done something to help them or to make them feel good.

4. Use personal evaluation sheets. These can be as simple or as complex as you desire. In this way, you can help children express feelings and see strengths/weaknesses in a non-threatening atmosphere.

5. Provide a wide variety of classroom experiences. Familiarity breeds self-confidence.

6. Implement a buddy system for this child.

7. Check into the home environment. See what is motivating this dependency.

8. Provide this child with simple, easy to accomplish tasks that allow for frequent success.

9. Provide self-correcting tasks so that the child may see his/her own errors first-hand.

10. Videotape your class in action and let the student, as well as the other students, actually see how he/she interacts in class.

MANAGEMENT PROBLEM:	*DESTRUCTIVENESS TO PROPERTY*

TEACHER'S
CONCERN:

There are certain students who show "carelessness" with other people's personal and/or school property, and still others who are willfully destructive. How can these aversive behaviors be impeded?

1. Try to make the punishment fit the crime (e.g., if a student breaks a pencil negligently, then it should be paid for or replaced if it was the school's property).

2. Demand that the student make some kind of mutually agreed upon retribution for his/her careless behavior.

3. Assign those students who destroy school property to special "work" details in and around the school (e.g., repainting walls that have graffiti on them, picking up trash, cleaning up the cafeteria, etc.).

4. Provide "constructive" classroom projects for students who get easily frustrated and/or overly anxious (e.g., build a classroom bookcase).

5. Give positive recognition and attention to those students when they are careful with other people's possessions and/or property (e.g., "That was very nice of you to pick up Susan's coat, Bill") .

6. Contact parents and/or inform administration when no viable solution can be reached.

7. Inform the police, juvenile court authorities, and other outside supportive agencies if there is an obvious and continuing pattern of destructive behavior. Be sure to consult your Teachers' Handbook before initiating any outside help so that you follow the appropriate procedures.

| MANAGEMENT PROBLEM: | *DEVELOPING LISTENING SKILLS* |

TEACHER'S CONCERN: How can listening skills be developed and improved?

WORKABLE OPTIONS:

1. Read to the class aloud and discuss details.

2. Play "What Did I Do?" Have children cover their eyes. Try sharpening a pencil, stir a spoon in a bowl, etc. Then ask children what they have heard.

3. Take time for listening to environmental sounds. Take the children outside and have them listen to the noises they hear and jot them down on their "listening" tablet.

4. Tap out rhythms and have the children repeat what they heard.

5. Give simple verbal instructions for the children to follow.

6. Play "Whisper Down the Lane" where the first child in a line is told something and this must be passed down the line. Usually the last person's interpretation does not resemble the original message!

7. Play restaurant. Children give orders and try to repeat the orders.

8. Teach children to try to eliminate as many distractions as possible.

9. Play repeating games using words or numerals. Child makes the statement: "For lunch I had ____" and each child adds to the list. All the added things must be repeated before the student adds his suggestion.

10. Ask the school nurse to check the hearing of those children who seem to have difficulty.

MANAGEMENT PROBLEM:	*DISRESPECT*
TEACHER'S CONCERN:	What can one do with a child who shows disrespect toward the teacher and the other students in the class?
WORKABLE OPTIONS:	

1. An immediate approach is to inform the child that this type of behavior is unacceptable and clearly explain the consequences if it occurs again.

2. Inform the parent(s) of the child's behavior and request their continual assistance in helping the child with this problem.

3. Have an individual conference with the child. Include the services of a counselor if it is available and have the child share his feelings concerning the problem and its possible solution.

4. Carefully select a child to team up with him/her in as many classroom activities and assignments as possible. Then, after a period of time, observe and evaluate any positive or negative change in the child.

5. A valuable experience in assisting a teacher with this and many other classroom problems is a course call "Teacher Effectiveness Training" or T.E.T. (Gordon). It shows one how to solve problems with students in the classroom without either person losing.

6. In order to gain respect, a teacher needs to model respect toward students, colleagues, and others in all situations. Sarcasm is the surest way to lose the respect of your students. It is unprofessional and uncalled for under any circumstances.

MANAGEMENT PROBLEM:	*DISRUPTION IN LEARNING CAUSED BY* *STUDENT ATTENDANCE IN MANDATED* *PROGRAMS*
TEACHER'S CONCERN:	How do you cope with the student who is involved in so many special programs in the school that he or she is always out of class?
WORKABLE OPTIONS:	

1. Try to remember that as the classroom teacher you will not be able to do "everything" for such a child. It is frustrating and nearly impossible to set such a goal for yourself.

2. Talk with the administrator about your specific concern so that he/she is aware of the limitations being set upon you.

3. Talk to the Resource Room teacher to see if you are able to get help from such personnel.

4. Create an extra time slot at the end of the day to help these students with material missed.

5. Use student tutors from upper grades to help these students.

6. Tape record core material. Use this as a basis for a learning center.

7. Make up fact sheets. Arrange parental cooperation for mastery of these skills using the fact sheets as a guideline.

8. Establish a buddy system for these students.

MANAGEMENT
PROBLEM: *DISRUPTIVE BEHAVIOR (FIGHTING, ARGUMENTS)*

TEACHER'S
CONCERN: What do you do with students who cannot get along with other students and continually get into fights and arguments?

WORKABLE
OPTIONS: 1. Evaluate the sources of frustration in the classroom that may contribute to a student getting into a fight. The student is influenced by the teacher, classmates, and the activities.

2. Check the type of discipline at home. Work with the parents to see if there can be some consistency.

3. In younger children, intervention only convinces the student that he/she will get attention for fighting. If the teacher attempts to direct these activities, the children will learn how to manage negative feelings more productively. See Glasser's "Reality Therapy" theory for specific guidelines on positive reinforcement.

4. Role play fighting situations and discuss what may happen if someone gets hurt, how to handle these situations more effectively and how to avoid these situations.

5. Take a student aside who has been fighting to find out what may have caused the fight. Never confront the student in front of the class.

6. Try to sit down with the students involved in the fight and see if a solution can be worked out.

7. Treat the student with respect and dignity to encourage his/her sense of responsibility for his/her own actions.

8. When discipline is necessary, be fair and consistent.

| MANAGEMENT PROBLEM: | *DRAWING ON DESK* |

MANAGEMENT PROBLEM: *DRAWING ON DESK*

TEACHER'S CONCERN: What do you do if a student is doing something other than his work such as playing under or drawing on his/her desk?

WORKABLE OPTIONS:

1. Establish rules for proper behavior during periods when students are at their desks.

2. Reinforce positive behavior of students who work at their desk properly.

3. Check to see that students have sufficient amount of work to do to keep them on task.

4. Vary your lessons so that students remain interested.

5. Collect pencils and crayons when they are not being used in your lesson, or be sure students clear their desks in preparation for the next activity.

6. Use hands-on projects as much as possible.

7. During regular class, give the students the chance to draw creatively as an interpretation of something they have learned.

8. Provide an interest center with drawing materials.

MANAGEMENT PROBLEM:	*DRUG ABUSE*
TEACHER'S CONCERN:	What should teachers do when they suspect and/or witness students involved with illegal drugs?
WORKABLE OPTIONS:	1. Refer the child to a doctor for a complete physical.

1. Refer the child to a doctor for a complete physical.

2. Have the child evaluated completely by the Child Study Team in your district.

3. Have the parents come in for a conference to discuss the child's home environment.

4. Speak to the class about drug problems and come up with solutions on how to help the student cope within the classroom environment.

5. Set up goals with the child that should be met within a certain time schedule.

6. Let the child work with one or more students to build relationships within the class.

7. Reward the child for positive behavior.

8. Encourage the child every day, it possible.

9. Follow the procedure delineated in your school handbook in regard to drug abuse.

10. Investigate agencies available to assist you in teaching your students about drugs.

MANAGEMENT PROBLEM:	*FAILURE TO ASK FOR HELP*

TEACHER'S CONCERN:

What do I do about a student who fails to ask for help on matters he/she does not fully understand in the curriculum or the classroom in general?

WORKABLE OPTIONS:

1. For various reasons, the student may not feel comfortable or confident about asking questions in certain classroom settings. Have an individual conference with the student to discuss the problem and together develop possible solutions.

2. If the student does not feel comfortable asking questions in the classroom setting, have him/her write the questions on a piece of paper or a 3x5 card you have available. Then when time permits, meet with the child individually to review the questions or provide general answers to the class because others may have the same questions.

3. Utilize other students in the classroom as resource persons to meet with the student and offer assistance. The student may be more apt to ask for help from a peer than from the teacher.

4. Consider the option of having the child evaluated by the Child Study Team for a possible learning disability or a health problem (poor hearing, poor vision, etc.).

5. Check to see if the student exhibits this behavior in other classrooms. If he/she does not, you may want to focus in on the way you relate to this student.

6. If available and practical, utilize the services of a counselor to assist the child in overcoming his/her reluctance to express him/herself in class.

7. Establish a chart listing all students and give recognition to those who ask questions in class. Emphasize that asking a question indicates intelligence, not stupidity.

MANAGEMENT PROBLEM:	*FIGHTING: NOT GETTING ALONG, NAME CALLING, ETC.*
TEACHER'S CONCERN:	What do you do with students who do not get along? These students exhibit behaviors such as fighting, name calling, ridiculing, pushing, and shoving at every opportunity.
WORKABLE OPTIONS:	1. Build self-confidence. Many books, articles, and material gleaned from surfing the Internet provide suggestions on what to do.

2. Use the "Magic Circle" technique or Glasser's "Reality Therapy," Cantor's "Assertive Discipline," or Skinner's "Behavior Modification" approaches.

3. Do role playing on how to handle a conflict situation. One skit should deal with socially acceptable behavior and another in correcting a socially unacceptable situation.

4. Discuss the importance of getting along in school, at home, and later in the working world.

5. Present situations concerning conflict resolutions. Have students break into groups to brainstorm socially acceptable solutions.

6. Check through films or videos available in the area of education. Look for materials dealing with social growth and conflict management.

7. Ignore the student's behavior unless safety warrants your immediate attention. Speak to the student privately later.

8. If the student is physically assaulting another student, break up the confrontation and allow the upset student to be isolated until he/she has sufficiently "cooled off." Follow school policy and report and record the incident for further referral.

| MANAGEMENT PROBLEM: | *FRUSTRATION* |

| TEACHER'S CONCERN: | How can you help a child deal with frustration after he/she has missed a part of a lesson due to illness or absence from the room for other reasons? |

WORKABLE OPTIONS:

1. Use the expertise of special teachers in your school and try to determine the cause of the frustration.

2. Discuss the problem with the student in privacy.

3. Provide the student with time-out to calm him/herself before returning to work. Such available resources as a quiet spot in the classroom or an interest corner with earphones and tapes are helpful.

4. Provide the student with a classroom tutor whom he/she can seek out to get information on the area of his/her frustration.

5. Rather than wait until a problem arises, be sure that the behavior expected in regard to entering and being part of the classroom is clearly defined.

6. Make every effort to schedule the student's time out of the classroom when the lessons in classroom do not affect him/her. For example, a student going to a Resource Room for individualized instruction in reading should go during the class reading period rather than during an art or science lesson.

7. Use the game "Class Applause" to assist in coping with this concern. This is played by having the students sit in a circle. Students concentrate on providing words of encouragement and affection for each other. Make sure that this student is included in the praise. Positive motivation and respect by peers is a real morale builder!

MANAGEMENT PROBLEM:	*HANDS-ON PROJECTS*
TEACHER'S CONCERN:	How can I obtain "hands-on projects or materials" for the students in my classroom?
WORKABLE OPTIONS:	

1. First, investigate the materials that may be located at your school. It is amazing what can be found in a storage room collecting dust. Ask the custodian, librarian, and principal about such materials and their possible location.

2. Consult with teachers who have more experience with such materials than you and your "mentor." They will have much to share with you.

3. Check the Internet, local museums, community libraries, and teacher supply stores for ideas.

4. Select "hands-on" material from catalogs and ask the administration to order them for you.

5. Take field trips and collect samples. Be creative and keep alert for free materials you can use.

6. Check out your county or state Educational Resource Materials Centers. In New Jersey it is called the EIC (Educational Improvement Center). These centers have samples of all varieties of curricular materials which you may borrow.

7. Send letters to major corporations to find out what materials they have available for you free of charge. Many businesses are very receptive to such requests.

8. Check out professional journals for materials and ideas ("The Instructor" and "New Teacher Advocate" published by Kappa Delta Pi, "Teacher Magazine," etc.). Use your college library resources for ideas found through the Internet.

MANAGEMENT PROBLEM:	*HOME INFLUENCES*
TEACHER'S CONCERN:	What do you do when home problems interfere with students being able to concentrate on school work and activities?
WORKABLE OPTIONS:	1. If a student is from a dysfunctional home, make sure you give him/her a friendly greeting, letting him/her know you are glad to see him/her.

2. If possible, request a parent conference. Try to discuss the academic problems the student is having. Be sure to plan this meeting with the parent(s) early in the school year and stress how important it is to work together to provide the educational experience possible. Explain clearly that if the child comes to school regularly, is well rested, and has had breakfast, you will be able to provide a maximum learning environment in the classroom. Ask if there is any way you can assist in lessening the child's stress from home problems.

3. If the child is not receiving breakfast at home or is not dressed properly (e.g., warm for winter) for school, call upon the school or communityresources. This includes checking for need of glasses or dentistry, which can affect the student's learning ability.

4. Use the services of the school counselor or the nurse as an open line of communication.

5. Minimize demands on student in regard to home assignments that would cause him/her hardship.

6. Follow up the first parent conference by calling or sending home notes describing positive actions of the student. This will help the child's sense of self-worth and increase his/her incentive to do even better in a safe and secure classroom.

40

MANAGEMENT PROBLEM:	*HOMEWORK*

TEACHER'S CONCERN: What can I do to get more students to do their homework consistently?

WORKABLE OPTIONS:

1. If practical, call the child's parent(s) the day homework is not completed. This way this student is aware of school and parental involvement when he/she doesn't fulfill a commitment at school.

2. Inform the parent(s) of the procedures you will use in assigning homework. Then the parent(s) will know what your expectations are and can be of assistance.

3. Make a sincere effort to "assign" homework that is meaningful and interesting.

4. Keep a record of what types of homework are returned more often than others. If any types of homework are favored, try to utilize them in future assignments.

5. Do not give homework for the sake of homework, but rather when it is necessary. This will give the assignments more meaning to you and the students.

6. Try not to give homework as punishment. This leads to the feeling that all homework is a negative experience.

7. Tell your class convincingly that homework is an earned privilege. The results of this may surprise you!

8. Be sure that you assign for homework only materials that the students fully understand and will be able to do. The parent(s) should not have to teach a skill to a student in order for him/her to complete the assignment.

41

MANAGEMENT PROBLEM:	*HOMEWORK POLICY AND PROCEDURE*

TEACHER'S
CONCERN:

What homework policy is fair and at the same time teaches children to assume the responsibility for homework assignments?

WORKABLE
OPTIONS:

1. Assign homework on a regular basis so that students are aware that homework is a part of your classroom routine. Try to avoid lengthy weekend assignments.

2. Make assignments brief: 15-20 minutes.

3. Assignments should involve review or reinforcement of skills covered in class that day.

4. Make assignments meaningful. Do not assign busy work for homework.

5. Discuss with your class the value of homework. Allow your students to air their complaints. Do not assume that students understand the reasoning for homework.

6. Use an assignment pad which requires your initials and parents' initials for students who do not return assignments. Make clear to the student that it will be his/her responsibility to write down the assignments. You initial the assignments as correct. Parents initial the assignments as completed.

7. To help students get assignments home in one piece and also to return work in good condition, encourage the use of plastic folders or book bags. Make folders or homework totes as a class art project. Mark all homework within 24 hours and return to students within that time frame.

8. Use progress charts as a way to encourage daily assumption of the responsibility of homework. Have meaningful rewards available for high achievers.

MANAGEMENT PROBLEM:	*HYPERACTIVITY - SHIFT IN ATTENTION*
TEACHER'S CONCERN:	What can be done for students who frequently shift their attention and/or interests in class?
WORKABLE OPTIONS:	

1. Assign the student some type of classroom responsibility that he/she looks forward to doing (e.g., collection of completed work, delivering messages, etc.).

2. Carefully arrange the student's work area to minimize classroom distractions (e.g., study carrels, room partitions, etc.).

3. Plan individual and/or group lessons that foster the development of analytical abilities in your students (e.g., a step-by-step approach in solving everyday problems).

4. Refer the student to a specialist and/or school nurse to check on visual and auditory deficits.

5. Provide your students with firm but fair classroom rules. Make sure you consistently adhere to the consequences.

6. Use social reinforcers frequently and as soon as possible (e.g., physical nearness or contact, a smile or frown, etc.) .

7. Prepare a variety of short lessons to maximize student attention and participation (e.g., manipulation exercises of fifteen to twenty minutes in duration).

8. Make suggestions to parents about the possibility of using various nutritional diets (e.g., Feingold diet).

9. Regularly incorporate "relaxation" techniques into the daily classroom routine and/or when the student is in need of them.

HYPERACTIVITY AND DISTRACTIBILITY

**TEACHER'S
CONCERN:**

How do you manage the "hyper" student and a student who is limited in the ability to screen out irrelevant stimuli?

**WORKABLE
OPTIONS:**

1. Employ hands-on activities.

2. Eliminate as many environmental distractions as possible.

3. Establish a well-defined work area for the child. This will help to limit outside activities that would detract from his/her concentration.

4. Use classroom aids such as headphones, tachistoscope, videos, etc. Provide for controlled exposures.

5. Pace activities realistically.

6. Incorporate gross motor skills into activities whenever possible.

7. Use bilateral activities, using hands and eyes in the lesson.

8. Make an obstacle course and have the students move through it at varying paces.

9. Use a timer. When the timer stops, students may have a short break. Never use a timer to speed up work, for it will cause tension and frustration rather than increase skill.

10. Have a "time out" period as a reward for a hyperactive child who has spent time doing correct activities.

MANAGEMENT PROBLEM:	*IMMATURE BEHAVIOR*
TEACHER'S CONCERN:	How can the incidence of immature behavior be decreased?
WORKABLE OPTIONS:	1. Evaluate your expectations. Be careful not to pressure or frustrate the children.

1. Evaluate your expectations. Be careful not to pressure or frustrate the children.

2. Ignore undesirable behavior.

3. Establish expected behaviors. Make list relevant, meaningful, minimal, and positive.

4. Identify problems in the classroom that lead to the exhibition of immature behaviors.

5. Check to see if your expectations are in line with the student's values.

6. Check for displaced feelings.

7. Check for problems at home.

8. If child exhibiting immature behaviors has been classified, check file for suggestions on how to cope with him/her.

9. Allow children to explain their reasons for use of immature behavior.

10. Consult with colleagues, your school counselor, or a member of the Child Study Team for ideas to cope with this problem..

IMPROVING LISTENING SKILLS

**TEACHER'S
CONCERN:**

What do you do with students who seem to be unable to listen and follow directions?

**WORKABLE
OPTIONS:**

1. Check informally for listening. Test students on memory for digits such as 1-7-10 and have students repeat them back to you.

2. Check informally to see if student can hear by dropping a coin behind him/her and see what happens. Cover your mouth with a piece of paper and determine if he/she can follow what you have said to do.

3. Give the students a series of directions: get the book, shut the door, look up at the light. As students improve, increase the complexity. (This can be played through the game "Simon Says".)

4. Check for sound location. Have students listen for a letter sound such as "d" and determine whether it comes at the beginning, middle, or end of the word.

5. Have students repeat directions or sentences.

6. Repeat various sequences of words and ask students to write them on a piece of paper in the proper order.

7. Try sequence stories. One student starts a story with a sentence. The next student repeats the first sentence and adds a new one, and so on.

8. Students tell simple jokes or riddles; other students try to remember and repeat them.

9. Play the game "In Grandmother's Attic." The first student starts by saying "In Grandmother's attic, I found" and gives a word beginning with "a". The next student repeats the "a" word and adds a word beginning with "b." Continue playing through the letter "z".

MANAGEMENT PROBLEM:	*INAPPROPRIATE BEHAVIOR DURING LUNCH AND/OR RECESS*
TEACHER'S CONCERN:	How can behavior during lunch or recess be improved?
WORKABLE OPTIONS:	

1. Establish rules for behavior in lunchroom and recess. Be reasonable with your rules.

2. Deny privileges to students who violate code of expected behavior (see Cantor's Assertive Discipline technique.).

3. Make the lunchroom/recess supervisor aware of your behavior code.

4. Role play situations where foolishness can lead to accidents in the lunchroom or playground.

5. Provide students with a variety of activities to do during recess.

6. Elect table monitors on a weekly basis. This can be done by seating arrangements. For example: In week #1 the child sitting in seat #1 on right side of table will be the monitor. Each week this will rotate to the next seat. This method can be implemented even in a cafeteria where seating is random choice.

7. Reverse the traditional lunch followed by recess routine and have recess first and then lunch. The children have expended a great deal of energy and are more capable of a less active time at lunch.

8. Set up a large screen TV in the cafeteria and show an appropriate movie (Disney or student choice). The local video store often will provide these free to schools! Choice of film can be a "reward" for good class behavior.

MANAGEMENT PROBLEM:	*INCOMPLETE CLASS ASSIGNMENTS AND/OR HOMEWORK*

TEACHER'S CONCERN:

Some students exhibit an unwillingness to complete class assignments and/or homework for a number of reasons (e.g., absenteeism, inefficient use of student time, unpreparedness, etc.). What can be provided for those students who demonstrate the above mentioned problem areas?

WORKABLE OPTIONS:

1. Give the student an assignment at the appropriate level of difficulty. Upon satisfactory completion, let the student "choose" an activity from a class list of reinforcing events (e.g., independent reading, drawing, homework, etc.).

2. Post a chart on the bulletin board stating what materials are to be brought to class each day.

3. Set up a "point" system reinforcing those behaviors that contribute to a student's preparedness. Exchange points earned for special individual and/or group activity (e.g., bring textbooks, notebooks, and supplies to class).

4. Provide the student with a "Term Course Contract." This agreement should carefully delineate what the student is expected to do in order to receive a certain grade and/or course credit. Also, it may be helpful to include "due" dates for long-range assignments, quizzes, major exams, etc.

5. Remind your students as often as needed when assignments are due.

6. Use "daily work contracts" for those students who need maximum structure (e.g., "I agree to complete *assignment* for the next *specified time*. Upon completion of my assignment, I will receive *award*). The teacher and student sign and date the contract.

MANAGEMENT PROBLEM:	*INCONSISTENCY*

TEACHER'S CONCERN:

What can I do with students who are inconsistent in routine matters?

WORKABLE OPTIONS:

1. Talk to the student to see if he/she knows and can say what the routine is.

2. If the student has problems after a considerable time, refer him/her to the Child Study Team. He/she may have a perceptual problem.

3. Be patient. Remind him/her of the routine. It takes some students more time than others to adjust to a routine.

4. Implement a behavior modification program.

5. Monitor this child frequently. Check to make sure he/she is doing what he/she is supposed to be doing.

6. Reinforce this child positively when he/she is consistent.

7. Involve the parents. See if they notice this at home. Help them establish a reward system for good days (i.e., days in which he/she followed the routine).

8. Examine the situation you consider "routine." Perhaps it is too complex or you have not allotted a sufficient amount of time for the students to understand it or learn it.

9. Examine your reaction to his/her inconsistency. Is the child being inconsistent to gain your attention? Is so, change your reaction.

10. Does your classroom routine actually reflect good classroom management or are you creating more problems by having such a rigid structure?

MANAGEMENT PROBLEM:	INDIVIDUAL ATTENTION TO SPECIAL NEEDS STUDENTS

TEACHER'S CONCERN:

A student needs individual attention in order to master a task and/or skill. How can a teacher personalize his/her instruction?

WORKABLE OPTIONS:

1. Use peer tutors to help students complete assignments.

2. Provide frequent individual conferences for the student in order to monitor his/her academic progress.

3. Notify parents about positive growth via Friday notes.

4. Set realistic goals for the student (e.g., modify class assignments when appropriate). Thoroughly review assigned work to ensure proper understanding.

5. Praise the student's achievements frequently in private and public.

6. Organize complex academic tasks into separate units and then place in sequential order for completion.

7. Prepare individual learning packets of work for the student to do. Ask him/her to return the assignments when completed for evaluation.

8. Use a variety of teaching materials in the classroom (e.g., taped books, videotaped programs, movies, slides, etc.).

9. Provide hands-on projects to help students establish academic concepts (e.g., model building).

10. Use self-correcting materials so that the student may receive immediate feedback (e.g., software).

MANAGEMENT PROBLEM:	*INDIVIDUALIZATION*
TEACHER'S CONCERN:	How can individual attention be given in a large classroom?
WORKABLE OPTIONS:	1. Use learning centers based on skills shown as deficient.

2. Tape record lessons intended for small group work.

3. Make up daily work packets for each child which contain handwriting and other simple review.

4. Try to use work that is self-correcting or has a key that a child can use.

5. Use student tutors from upper grades for routine work, while you attend to special problems that occur.

6. Implement the use of educational TV.

7. Team teach when possible to provide more efficient use of time.

8. Use audiovisual materials: language master, Systems 80, tachistoscope.

9. Evaluate grouping arrangements for better utilization of time.

10. Implement individual prescription instruction (IPI) system.

11. Be flexible and be willing to change direction when individual needs are evident.

12. Have a grading system so the student can check his/her work and work at his/her own pace.

MANAGEMENT PROBLEM:	*INDIVIDUALIZATION: DEPENDENCY*
TEACHER'S CONCERN:	What do you do with a student who demands your individual attention for most of the work period and seems to feel he/she cannot proceed without your personal direction?
WORKABLE OPTIONS:	1. Establish fixed goals for the students and a fixed amount of time to accomplish the goals. Be sure your directions are clear.

2. Institute a "buddy" system. Students will work together to complete work.

3. Place directions on a tape . The student who has difficulty remembering the directions can play the tape back as many times as necessary.

4. Use inviting learning centers for students who have completed their seat work.

5. Check with the appropriate school personnel to see if this child has a learning problem or lacks processing skills.

6. Make it a policy to send home a note to parents concerning their child's performance for the week. This can be a simple check off sheet that reflects progress. Encourage parents to reward good progress.

7. Use a timer. When the timer is running, students are to work at their seats. When timer goes off, the students may take a short break. Never use timer for the general class to complete work. This may stress students unnecessarily and prevent them from doing their work.

8. Provide access to varied practice sheets that the students may use when they have finished their work.

MANAGEMENT PROBLEM:	*INTERRUPTIONS FROM ADMINISTRATION*

TEACHER'S CONCERN:

What can I do about the constant interruptions from the office and pupils sent from other classes with messages?

WORKABLE OPTIONS:

1. First, ask other teachers if they feel the same as you do concerning classroom interruptions. This will ensure that there is an accurate focus on the effect of this problem.

2. At the next faculty or liaison meeting, ask that the problem be discussed and that possible solutions be offered and analyzed for feasibility.

3. If for some reason you are hesitant to confront the administration or fellow teachers with this concern, type your thoughts, feelings, and possible solutions on a letter and submit it to the administration for suggestions and clarification.

4. When a child interrupts your class with a note, read it and then tell the student to tell the 'sender" that you will respond to the message at lunch or another time (unless the answer is "yes" or "no").

5. Ask the principal to inform teachers in the special areas to adhere to their predetermined schedules so that the classroom teachers can better plan their day and not be interrupted at an unexpected time.

6. When testing, place a sign on your door that states "PLEASE DO NOT DISTURB – TESTING."

7. Request that the office make announcements on the public address system only at the same scheduled times of the day (e.g., morning announcements, closing of school announcements).

8. Prepare a plan that will facilitate communication without interruption.

MANAGEMENT PROBLEM:	*INTERRUPTIONS DURING GROUP WORK*
TEACHER'S CONCERN:	How can one cope with children who interrupt the teacher during group work with legitimate questions regarding their individual assigned task?
WORKABLE OPTIONS:	1. Appoint group captains. Use more conscientious students for this job. They can help to answer questions for you.

1. Appoint group captains. Use more conscientious students for this job. They can help to answer questions for you.

2. Use a stop/go sign to indicate when you are available for questioning. These can be purchased at any teacher supply store.

3. Between sessions of group work, give students some free time to seek your attention. Take a snack break.

4. Discuss with your class reasons for the need for uninterrupted group sessions.

5. Reward the class for periods of uninterrupted work.

6. Give students guidance on how to skip areas of uncertainty and move on to work that they know so they do not spend all of their time waiting for the helper or for the break time to talk to the teacher.

7. Try to give equal time to each group so that the students at their seats are not expected to work for unrealistic extended periods. The younger the class, the shorter the period should be.

MANAGEMENT PROBLEM;	*LACK OF COMMON SENSE IN BEHAVIOR*
TEACHER'S CONCERN:	What can I do to improve common sense knowledge of my students?
WORKABLE OPTIONS:	1. Have a conference with the student to help give examples of how using common sense is important in everyday classroom routine.

1. Have a conference with the student to help give examples of how using common sense is important in everyday classroom routine.

2. Make sure the student thinks carefully before he/she says or writes something in class.

3. Talk to the parents about the problem. They can help the child develop common sense skills at home.

4. Develop a unit within the class. Have a group identify "common sense" knowledge. Follow up with classification of how common sense is used in everyday activity.

5. Discuss how using common sense is a way to be safe (e.g., provide examples of how common sense on the playground keeps a child from getting hurt).

6. Role play activities that demonstrate use of common sense reactions to everyday school situations.

7. Have students identify how classroom rules reflect common sense.

MANAGEMENT PROBLEM:	*LACK OF DISCIPLINE AT HOME: Part 1*

TEACHER'S CONCERN:	How can you deal with children with parents who aren't supportive of school recommended disciplinary steps at home?

WORKABLE OPTIONS:

1. Be aware of the fact that each home has its own management system and there will be times when the program of the school may conflict with the value system and procedures of the home. The school can try to make changes but will not always succeed. Teachers have an obligation to try and should understand that lack of success is not necessarily the same as failure.

2. Implement a behavior modification program (see Krumboltz, Skinner, Thomas) to be used with students needing structured discipline.

3. Bring the child's parent(s) into the problem in a positive manner. Ask their advice and share their concerns. Invite them in for conferences for which you are thoroughly prepared with anecdotal notes concerning the child's behavior. Involve the principal, Child Study Team, and/or department heads if necessary to provide support for yourconcern.

4. Use the technique of sending home daily behavior reports to parents who have agreed to cooperate. Always begin these reports on a positive note. This personalized communication demonstrates to the parents that you are willing to go "that extra mile" for their child even though you have many children in your class.

5. Develop a positive relationship with the home by contacting parents to provide information of good behavior rather than just negative reports.

56

MANAGEMENT	
PROBLEM:	*LACK OF DISCIPLINE AT HOME: Part 2*

TEACHER'S
CONCERN: What can a teacher do to reach parents of undisciplined students?

WORKABLE
OPTIONS:

1. Be sure that if you deny the student privileges in school as the result of behavior that this discipline relates directly to the rule violated. Discipline must he a learning experience. (See Cantor's Assertive Discipline program.) Give parents information on the discipline program you are using so they understand the process and procedures.

2. Play the game "What is ahead for me?" The procedure is as follows: Discuss the consequences of the student's behavior. List future happenings that might occur if he/she improves. List items that may occur if he/she continues to misbehave. Share this with the child's parents.

3. Constantly reexamine your relationship with the child and parent. Are you being overly sensitive? Are you "picking on" one child? Have you stigmatized this child because of the reputation of his/her siblings?

4. Review the child's cumulative folder to see if there is any indication that his/her behavior is characteristic of this child throughout his/her school experience.

5. Keep anecdotal records that note when behavior occurs. Share with the parent(s) whether he/she works better in the morning than in the afternoon or what seems to trigger his/her negative behavior in class. Ask if anything at home stimulates this behavior (e.g., lack of sleep, no breakfast, etc.).

MANAGEMENT PROBLEM:	*LACK OF INTEREST IN ACADEMICS*

TEACHER'S CONCERN: How can you deal with a student who places emphasis on sports rather than academics?

WORKABLE OPTIONS:

1. Ask members of the honor society to speak to your class. Have them stress prestige and value of learning.

2. Call the parents. Explain that such an attitude will hinder progress. Stress the need for them to work with you in a team approach to change this attitude.

3. Obtain books for the student to read that give biographical data on outstanding athletes who were successful academically in college and became doctors, lawyers, etc., when their athletic careers ended.

4. Reward high academic achievers through contests and competition in classroom work.

5. Be aware that teachers must deal with parents' value systems and be accepting of these values.

6. Us the game "Goalpost" as an incentive. Set up a goalpost on the bulletin board. Each day set a goal for each child. As he/she completes goals set, he/she crosses over the goalpost. If goals aren't completed, discuss reasons that prevented success.

7. Work with the teachers involved with sport activities to stimulate better student performance in academcs. Encourage them to show how they need to know math, science, art, etc., in order to follow a play or participate in a sports activity.

8. Relate learning situations to sport events (e.g., scores and running distances to mathematics, past records in sports to history).

MANAGEMENT
PROBLEM: *LACK OF MOTIVATION: Part 1*

TEACHER'S
CONCERN: What do you do with students who lack motivation,
have a very negative attitude toward school, and come
to class unprepared?

WORKABLE
OPTIONS: 1. Do everything possible to make sure the physical
condition of the student has been met. Has he/she eaten
breakfast, had enough rest, see the board clearly, hear
clearly, etc.?

2. Make your classroom interesting and stimulating
to the students. Make your lessons inviting and
challenging so students want to find out what will
come next!

3. Show your students that you take an interest in
them. Show that you like them and they belong in
your classroom.

4. Make your lesson an experience that will allow the
student to gain in self esteem because he/she is
successful.

5. Make goals that are challenging but attainable.

6. Take advantage of the student's interest and
formulate some lessons around them.

8. When developing practice worksheets, use the
student's names and some thing you know about
them to teach a concept (e.g., "Susan expressed her
enjoyment regarding her trip to Disney World"
when identifying parts of speech).

9. Send home weekly reports to parents. Encourage
parents to reward for high motivation.

10. Use the concept of working together to encourage
each other such as cooperative learning groups.

11. Have students chart their behavior for a week.

MANAGEMENT PROBLEM:	*LACK OF MOTIVATION: Part 2*
TEACHER'S CONCERN:	What methods can I use to motivate my students' interest in learning?
WORKABLE OPTIONS:	1. Use incentives in the classroom such as prizes, stars, and rewards for completing assignments on time to reinforce motivation toward accomplishment.

1. Use incentives in the classroom such as prizes, stars, and rewards for completing assignments on time to reinforce motivation toward accomplishment.

2. Get to know each child as an individual to gain insight into strengths and interests.

3. Have monthly conferences with students discussing work habits, motivation, behavior, etc.

4. Have a real purpose in the school work you assign to your students so it relates to their needs.

5. Assist the student in setting realistic goals.

6. Don't always point out errors on a student's work, but show how improvement can be made on the finished product.

7. Provide editing time when you work one-to-one with students in perfecting their creative work.

8. Show enthusiasm while you teach because the teacher is the key to motivation in the classroom.

9. Develop special projects for the child whose interests have not yet been tapped by the school routine.

10. Create special recognition through "student of the month" or "star for the day." See "Ticket Program" in Section II.

60

MANAGEMENT PROBLEM:	*LACK OF RESPECT*
TEACHER'S CONCERN:	What do you do with students who show a lack of respect for adults, peers, their belongings, and property of others?
WORKABLE OPTIONS:	

1. The teacher should practice the 3 R's: respect, responsibility, and reciprocity.

2. Role play situations where there is lack of respect. Example: Someone fails a test and others make fun of that person. Follow with group analysis and discussion of situation and alternative actions.

3. Clearly state the reasons for respect for other people's property. Publicly acknowledge those demonstrating respect for other's property so peers can model their behavior.

4. Show videos dealing with respect and then discuss them. See Guidance Associates materials . Obtain materials from your county audio library.

5. Don't make unrealistic requests, dictate rules without explanations, or give ultimatums that will give students a boundary that they might be tempted to break because they feel it is unreasonable.

6. Listen to each student. Never automatically assume you know what the student is going to say in explaining his/her actions.

7. Show that even though as the teacher you are in charge of the class, you respect the student and expect respect in return.

8. Never give idle sarcastic threats! (e.g., "How many times have I told you to sit down? I am going to have to take away your recess time for the semester unless you behave.")

61

MANAGEMENT PROBLEM:	*LACK OF SELF-ESTEEM OF STUDENT REQUIRED TO RECEIVE OUTSIDE CLASSROOM AID*
TEACHER'S CONCERN:	How can I make students feel better about themselves and their self-worth and still have them participate in outside instructional services?
WORKABLE OPTIONS:	1. Let the student know that the additional help is there for him/her to improve on his/her academic achievement and is not a punishment. Tell him/her there are many students who receive this aid and that is because they have potential and are special.

1. Let the student know that the additional help is there for him/her to improve on his/her academic achievement and is not a punishment. Tell him/her there are many students who receive this aid and that is because they have potential and are special.

2. Encourage the student on his/her progress and give abundant praise.

3. Reward the student appropriately for his success in the special instructional program.

4. Provide many opportunities for the student to succeed while he/she is participating in regular class activities so that he/she feels he/she belongs.

5. Have a conference with the parent(s) so they will support and encourage the student at home to try to improve the skills for which he/she is receiving extra help.

6. Use the services of the school guidance counselor if you feel lack of self-esteem is a major concern.

7. Develop a program for teachers and students explaining the merits of out-of-class special instruction to give it a positive place in the school curriculum.

8. Set up a bulletin board for display of good work and include the work done well by students attending special instructional classes.

MANAGEMENT PROBLEM:	*LEARNING CENTERS*
TEACHER'S CONCERN:	I would like to use learning centers in the classroom. Where can I get information in this area?
WORKABLE OPTIONS:	1. First, observe a teacher who has successfully implemented learning centers in the classroom. This information and permission can be obtained from the administration.

2. Plan a visit to a learning center in your state. You can find out where they are by contacting your district and/or state educational offices. In New Jersey there are Educational Improvement Centers (EIC) located at colleges and special buildings. The State Department of Education in Trenton can provide you with specific locations. These centers have workshops, literature, and complete learning center materials that can be borrowed for classroom use.

3. There are many books available at your local library that provide details on the development and utilization of learning centers. They are excellent sources for ideas and procedures that have worked successfully in the classroom.

4. Complete materials can be purchased at teacher supply stores to make up an interest center. Once you get the idea, it is easy to develop your own models.

5. Build an interest center reflecting a curriculum area as a classroom project.

6. If the space is available, designate a room in the school where teachers can display and share learning centers that they have purchased or made. This would be similar to a "Science Fair" but would actually be a "Learning Center Fair" that could be on display for parents as well.

MANAGEMENT PROBLEM:	*LISTENING*

TEACHER'S CONCERN: What do I do with students who will not listen?

WORKABLE OPTIONS:

1. Have the student's hearing tested.

2. Have the student's auditory perception tested by the school's learning consultant or psychologist.

3. If results from options 1 and 2 are both negative, assume that the student does not choose to listen or may have an attention deficit.

4. Is the student daydreaming or preoccupied with something else? If so, repeat what you have asked of him/her.

5. Discuss with the student his/her listening problem. See what is on his/her mind.

6. If there is no open relationship between you and the student, find another person with whom he/she can relate (e.g., the school counselor, another teacher, or one of his friends).

7. Do not consistently repeat yourself. Attach a consequence if your directions are not followed after saying it once. Be sure to speak clearly and be consistent in enforcing your listening rules.

8. Discuss your expectations and consequences in the beginning of the school year. Speak clearly and precisely.

9. Try not to give too many directions at the same time. Some students cannot retain a long sequence of directions.

10. Be sensitive and listen to the students so that they will model your behavior.

64

MANAGEMENT PROBLEM:	*LISTENING SKILLS DEVELOPMENT*

TEACHER'S CONCERN:	Is there any way to improve listening skills in the classroom?

WORKABLE OPTIONS:

1. Contact the reading specialist in your district. This person can be a valuable resource for providing or sharing techniques and materials in the development of listening skills with the students.

2. Especially in the upper grades, explain to the students that they will be evaluated by a test after any group discussion. This will give the students incentive to use and develop listening skills.

3. In your closure after each lesson, be sure you review with your student what they have learned in that lesson so they will see the need for listening attentively.

4. Be sure that you and the students know what is meant by "listening skills" and are able to develop an understanding of the important basic facts of a lesson.

5. Attend professional workshops that provide information on developing listening skills in your classroom.

6. In the lower grades, ask the students to write down in list form as many facts or ideas they can remember after a class discussion.

7. Offer listening skill awards for students who demonstrate progress in this area. Recognize publicly during the class sessions when a student shows he/she has listened and interpreted a concept correctly and thoughtfully during a class activity or discussion.

MANAGEMENT PROBLEM:	*LOW FRUSTRATION TOLERANCE*
TEACHER'S CONCERN:	How can teachers successfully challenge their students but still remain within the limits of their frustration range?
WORKABLE OPTIONS:	1. Provide many different opportunities for students to cope with gradual doses of mild frustration and increased difficulty.

1. Provide many different opportunities for students to cope with gradual doses of mild frustration and increased difficulty.

2. Plan activities that ensure more success than failure for students (e.g., independent projects of their own choosing).

3. Respond to the student's frustration by reducing or changing performance demands (e.g., reinforce partially correct responses, shorten assignments, etc.) .

4. Organize complex tasks into separate parts, and then present the material in a logical sequential order for completion.

5. Make every effort to give positive feedback to students who have successfully completed their assignments.

6. Personalize academic instruction for those students who need additional help in alleviating some of their frustrations.

7. Try to anticipate when the student will become frustrated, and then change the activity accordingly.

8. Allow the student to work at his/her own pace.

9. Help the student to develop a positive self-image.

10. Refer the student to the appropriate school personnel if the problem persists.

66

MANAGEMENT PROBLEM:	*LYING TO AUTHORITY FIGURES*

TEACHER'S
CONCERN:

When confronted with students who are obviously lying, what are some viable options for handling the situations?

WORKABLE
OPTIONS:

1. Realize that what is dishonest for mature adults may not be for the student's peers. Plan activities that improve the student's perception of honesty and how to implement it in everyday situations.

2. Provide consistent discipline and positive but firm classroom rules.

3. Give opportunities for students to express their negative feelings (e.g., private conferences, class discussions, written assignments, etc., as general class activities) .

4. Use activities that will build feelings of mutual respect with peers and/or adults (e.g., group projects involving work in the community).

5. Be calm and rational when you know a student is not telling the truth by not making it the center of the classroom discussion. GIVE POSITIVE ATTENTION WHEN THE STUDENT DISPLAYS COURAGE TO BE HONEST (e.g.,"You impressed me when you acknowledged that you were involved in that incident").

6. If a student is being defensive when lying, it may be result of years of punitive discipline. Instead of punishing him/her severely, provide positive discipline techniques that will not force more responsibility on the student than he/she can handle (e.g., write a short theme on the "Positive effects of admitting when you are wrong").

7. For students who obviously lie to impress their peers, praise them whenever they are being honest.

MANAGEMENT PROBLEM:	*MISUSE OF TEACHERS' OR AIDES' TIME*
TEACHER'S CONCERN:	What do you do when students constantly come up to the teacher's desk for help?
WORKABLE OPTIONS:	

1. Make a tape recording with animal sounds. Assign each group of five students an animal sound. When they hear their sound on the recording. it is their opportunity to come up to the teacher's desk for questions, to tell her a story, etc.

2. On a daily basis, provide a short period of time when students sit in a circle and discuss questions, stories, or problems. Encourage students to save discussion throughout the day for this circle time.

3. Make a schedule that provides a short span of time for each student to discuss concerns with the teacher.

4. Discourage students from coming up to the teacher's desk at inappropriate times.

5. Provide an "instant gratification" sheet where a student may write down briefly his/her immediate need. The teacher can scan this quickly and respond to those who need immediate attention between groups or at convenient times.

6. Provide classroom helpers to respond to questions about the independent work students are doing. (See *Attention-Seeking Well-Behaved Student.*)

7. Provide clearly stated rules so the students do not need to "ask the teacher" for everything (e.g., a pass for the bathroom; availability of paper, pencils, extra worksheets; etc., which can be used by the students without asking the teacher).

MANAGEMENT PROBLEM:	*MOTIVATION THROUGH SEATWORK*

TEACHER'S CONCERN:

How can students with ability be motivated to complete seatwork even though they say "I can't !"?

WORKABLE OPTIONS:

1. Check to see if there are any physical reasons for the student's inability to handle independent work. The school nurse or family doctor can look for visual, auditory, perceptual problems, low energy level, or lack of ability to concentrate.

2. Plan activities that revolve around student interest.

3. Insure success in the independent work given the students. It should be neither too difficult nor too easy to complete.

4. Allow children to express their likes and dislikes in regard to independent work. Make your standards known so they are fully aware of what you consider satisfactory work.

5. Provide space for the students to establish interest centers, encouraging those students who lack motivation to develop centers illustrating their hobbies and talents.

6. Provide a classroom that is attractive and stimulating with resource materials easily accessible.

7. Reward the students who show progress so that every child in the room has an opportunity to be rewarded.

8. Establish goals with each child and reinforce with frequent review and personal interaction.

9. Evaluate (mark) children's work as quickly as possible in order to eliminate frustration and prevent reinforcement of erroneous concepts.

MANAGEMENT PROBLEM:	*NAME CALLING - SOMETIMES RACIAL*

TEACHER'S CONCERN:

What do you do with students who will call other students names, sometimes with racial overtones?

WORKABLE OPTIONS:

1. Show videos depicting various cultures and discuss variation in each. Emphasize that being different is not bad.

2. Role play name calling situations and have a discussion afterward.

3. Assign groups of students to a different culture. Using cooperative learning groups, have students develop a group skit to be presented at a "Multicultural Fair" with each group showing their culture's dress, food, language, etc.

4. Establish rules concerning name calling, coupled with strict consequences for disobeying these rules.

5. Reward students for not responding aggressively to other students calling them names.

6. Provide activities that illustrate the unfairness of prejudice and name calling such as: (a) having only blue-eyed students participating in a favorite activity (b) allowing only boys to get a drink, etc. This shows the unfairness of bias. Let children explore the multitude of ways they can be "classified" and the unfairness of this.

7. Ask the students to report on real-life situations different from their own. (What would it be like to live on the streets? What would be different if you lived in Alaska?, etc.) Develop presentations for the class.

MANAGEMENT PROBLEM:	*NEGATIVE RESPONSE TO REQUESTS AND RULES*
TEACHER'S CONCERN:	When confronted with students who are negative about rational requests and/or rules, what are some possible options for teachers?
WORKABLE OPTIONS:	1. Try to use these guidelines when establishing classroom rules: a) Involve your class in making up the rules. b) State the rules positively. c) Rules should be brief and to the point. d) Review rules periodically with the class. 2. Arrange private conferences with students to discuss the problem in depth. 3. Ask the student(s) to write down the disturbing behavior in a class log book. Have him/her write some appropriate alternative ways of responding to negativity for future reference. 4. Provide choices to students in order to minimize negative reactions (e.g., "Would you rather stay an extra ten minutes and finish the exercise before lunch, or go to lunch now and finish it when you come back?"). 5. Try to produce frequent positive interaction in the class (e.g., praise, group projects, discussions, etc.) . 6. Make sure students clearly understand what is expected from them. (In some cases, it's the student's confusion that causes oppositional behavior.) 7. Handle difficult students individually outside the classroom, so that there is less of a chance of others getting involved. 8. Contact parents, the principal, and/or counselor to discuss the student's inappropriate behavior.

MANAGEMENT PROBLEM:	*NERVOUS HABITS IN CLASSROOM*
TEACHER'S CONCERN:	What do you do with a student who has a habit of chewing on erasers, crayons, and pencils?
WORKABLE OPTIONS:	1. Evaluate if there is too much pressure being placed on the student causing him/her to develop a nervous habit.

1. Evaluate if there is too much pressure being placed on the student causing him/her to develop a nervous habit.

2. Have a parent conference to find out if there are any stress situations taking place at home.

3. Have a student conference to discuss concerns and the fact that the habit annoys others.

4. Provide rewards for the student who conforms to the rules and shows improvement in controlling this behavior.

5. If pencils or crayons are too tempting for the student, collect them after activities are completed.

6. Establish a "Behavior Modification" program (Skinner) to wean the student away from these habits.

7. Seek out the professional expertise of the school psychologist.

MANAGEMENT PROBLEM:	*NOISY WORK HABITS*

TEACHER'S CONCERN: What do you do with a few students who constantly call out or talk loudly while other students are working quietly? How can the noise level of the classroom be controlled most efficiently?

WORKABLE OPTIONS:

1. Provide frequent breaks and a change of pace.

2. Reward students for not calling out in class.

3. Provide learning centers that students may go to after completing their work.

4. Separate a constant talker to the back of the classroom with a study carrel.

5. Maintain a progress chart on the bulletin board recording the positive independent work of students.

6. For questions, have students hold up a sign with a question mark on it which you can see and respond to.

7. Provide individual task cards which students will be able to do when their assignment is completed.

8. Play soft music as a reward when students are working in non-academic areas and have kept the class noise level down.

9. Combine desirable activities with less desirable activities. If an activity holds the children's interest, less talking will take place.

10. Clarify reasons for the benefits of a quiet work time.

11. Establish clear rules during seatwork and enforce them consistently.

MANAGEMENT
PROBLEM: *NOT DRESSED FOR GYM*

TEACHER'S
CONCERN: What can I do if a student does not attend
                       detention when he/she does not dress for gym and that
                       is a school rule?

WORKABLE
OPTIONS: 1. Have another student walk with him/her to the
                       detention room to make sure he/she gets there.

                       2. Take away certain privileges if the student cuts
                       detention.

                       3. Have a conference with the parents of the student
                       to explain that the student is not dressing for gym
                       and refuses to go to detention.

                       4. Report the problem to the principal and see if
                       she/he can help out.

                       5. Give the student extra work if he/she is not
                       prepared for gym.

                       6. Discuss the problem with the student in private to
                       see what his/her reasons are for not being prepared.

                       7. Talk to the gym teacher to see if he/she has some
                       insight into the problem.

                       8. If it is determined it is an economic problem (child
                       cannot afford gym outfit), see the school nurse
                       about contacting a local service agency that will
                       provide this for the student (community centers,
                       service agencies, etc.).

MANAGEMENT PROBLEM:	*OFF-TASK BEHAVIOR*

TEACHER'S CONCERN:

What do I do with students who are not doing what they are supposed to do? These students will talk and play, waste time, move about the room, etc., rather than work on class assignments.

WORKABLE OPTIONS:

1. Discuss expectations with the class at the beginning of the year.

2. Discuss expectations in private with students who are having difficulty keeping on task.

3. Write the task on the board. If daily seatwork assignments are given, write this in the same location daily so students get into the habit of looking for their assignments.

4. Hold each student responsible for the assignment. Check work individually on a daily basis. The student will be more likely to do it if he/she knows you will definitely check to see if it's done.

5. Attach consequences to tasks undone.

6. Attach a consequence for being off-task (talking, walking around, playing).

7. Examine the cause. Is the task too easy? Is it too difficult? Are you inconsistent in enforcing the consequences? Is the consequence not severe enough to discourage this behavior?

8. Employ a firm behavior modification program.

9. Contact the parents. Try an at-home reward system with them. Send home daily reports concerning the student's behavior.

10. Have the child checked for a potential hearing problem or a health problem that makes it difficult for him/her to sit quietly for extended periods.

MANAGEMENT	
PROBLEM:	*PRESTIGE: EQUAL VALUE TO ALL SUBJECTS*

TEACHER'S
CONCERN:

Other subject area teachers indicate that art is not as important as other subjects, and this attitude is transferred to the students. How can I make teachers and students understand the importance of art as part of the school curriculum?

WORKABLE
OPTIONS:

1. Explain to the students the importance of art and the people who have contributed in the history of art.

2. Ask the principal if you can give a presentation to faculty regarding the role art plays in their teaching of academic subjects.

3. Have art lessons that are appropriate for your students' needs as well as complementary to the academic work in which they are currently involved.

4. Work with the principal in scheduling your classes so they do not frustrate other staff members.

5. Bring in video, films, and projects; suggest field trips to museums; and display your students' art throughout the school to demonstrate the role of art in everyday experiences.

6. Help the classroom teachers with their bulletin board displays. You will become endeared to them for this offer alone!

MANAGEMENT PROBLEM:	*PAPER WORK*
TEACHER'S CONCERN:	How do I deal more effectively with paper work?
WORKABLE OPTIONS:	1. When developing assignments and tests, keep in mind the evaluation process. How difficult will they be to grade?

2. Train capable students to do some of the paper work. They could save you a considerable amount of time by placing papers in alphabetical order, filing, separating different materials, and simple grading using a grading template.

3. If, in your opinion, an unnecessary amount of paper work is coming from the office, request a liaison meeting to evaluate and perhaps reduce or combine the forms requested.

4. Ask the administration to schedule a workshop where fellow teachers share their techniques of dealing with paper work.

5. Develop some basic forms you can use to keep records of student progress.

6. Have students keep a work folder that can be used to store their work and provide a good source of comparative analysis of their progress throughout the year as well as points of information for parent-teacher conferences.

MANAGEMENT PROBLEM:	*PARENTAL INVOLVEMENT WITH THEIR CHILDREN*
TEACHER'S CONCERN:	How do I get the parents of my students involved in their children's welfare in the classroom environment?
WORKABLE OPTIONS:	1. Periodically telephone the parents and tell them about the child's progress in all areas and the things that must be worked on.

1. Periodically telephone the parents and tell them about the child's progress in all areas and the things that must be worked on.

2. Have the parents use reinforcement procedures in the home and give some suggestions on how this is done at your first "Open House."

3. Send out a letter to all your students before the school year, welcoming them to your class and presenting a brief synopsis of the major areas of learning that you plan to cover during that school year.

4. Communicate with the parents on a regular basis other than the report card. Monthly or weekly updates are helpful. Personalize these notices if possible if there is a problem or something especially productive has happened with a particular student.

5. Make the parents feel welcome and free to visit your classroom at any time.

6. Read and get ideas from many professional books and journals regarding parent-teacher involvement.

7. Visit the child's home if there is extended absence or you have never met the parent, to show that you are willing to go that extra mile to provide the best possible learning environment for each child in your class.

MANAGEMENT	
PROBLEM:	*PARENT SUPPORT PROCEDURES*

TEACHER'S
CONCERN: Is it possible to increase parental support for the classroom teacher?

WORKABLE
OPTIONS:

1. Publish a monthly newspaper, co-authored by the teacher and the students, to inform the parents of what is occurring in the classroom and to share the exceptional and creative work of the students. Make every effort to see that all students are included by the end of the school year.

2. On PTA meeting evenings, open your classroom one-half hour before the announced starting time and welcome your parents to attend so they can see your classroom and talk to you. This is especially helpful for parents who have more than one student in the same school .

3. At the beginning of the school year, inform the parent(s) what you plan to accomplish with their children in the coming months. Be absolutely clear in stating their role and responsibility. Assure them that parental involvement is essential if the goals are to be fulfilled.

4. Attend workshops or seminars that give you ideas on how to improve parent and teacher interaction.

5. Ask the administration to establish parental involvement as a district goal and state that clearly in the calendar distributed at the beginning of the school year.

6. Send a questionnaire to the parents asking for their ideas on how to increase parental involvement and support in the classroom.

7. Provide parenting workshops for parents.

8 Establish a Community Advisory Board that will meet monthly to review school policy decisions.

MANAGEMENT PROBLEM:	*PLANNING AND INNOVATION*
TEACHER'S CONCERN:	How can I be innovative and follow strict planning at the same time? When using a technique new to me and/or my students, it is difficult to estimate the length of the lesson or the follow-up that will be necessary. Yet, if observed, I am expected to be doing exactly what the lesson plan states.
WORKABLE OPTIONS:	1. Block out a section in the weekly lesson plan that will be used to try new teaching techniques or implement any new idea. Have an explanation written into the plans stating that the factors, such as time, associated with this lesson may not be accurate or known because of the nature of the lesson.

2. Keep the administrator well informed when you are trying a new approach or technique. In this way, he/she will have a better understanding of the lesson if you happen to be observed. In fact, he/she most certainly will be supportive of your "adventure" into new horizons so he/she may make a special effort to observe your new idea and give positive and helpful feedback!

3. When trying a new technique have the principal, if practical, be involved as a resource for ideas and recommendations. In this way when changes are made within the lesson plan, cooperation with the principal will more likely occur.

4. Explain, orally or in written form, that if an increase in professional growth is expected from the teaching staff, there must be more flexibility in the district's policy toward "lesson planning."

5. Share your concerns and ideas with another teacher who is working on the same topic or unit. Find out how he/she has fared and what has been a successful time frame or the procedures she/he has found worked most productively.

MANAGEMENT PROBLEM:	*PLAYGROUND INTERACTION*

TEACHER'S CONCERN:

What do you do with the student who keeps the students in turmoil on the playground because he/she keeps making them choose sides, won't play with certain students, has a complaint about all decisions being made, is overly aggressive, etc.?

WORKABLE OPTIONS:

1. Establish rules for expected behavior during playground periods.

2. Establish with the person in charge of playground what behavior you expect from your students during recess.

3. Follow through with corrective behavior on playground.

4. Praise students for good reports of behavior on playground.

5. Isolate students for misconduct (e.g., sit five minutes on curb to settle down).

6. Show a film on safety on the playground and discuss safety rules with your class.

7. Teach students games that can be played on the playground.

8. Indicate areas for specific play activities (e.g., jump rope, basketball boundaries, baseball boundaries, racing games, etc.) so there is no overlapping or conflict.

9. Introduce the "Assertive Discipline" (Cantor) program to be used for playground management.

10. Select a weekly "playground monitor" from your class to help manage appropriate behavior of your students as a model for others.

| MANAGEMENT PROBLEM: | *POOR ADJUSTMENT TO CHANGE IN ENVIRONMENT* |

| TEACHER'S CONCERN: | Some students have difficulty coping with new and/or unfamiliar tasks or situations, and may even attempt to avoid them. How can a teacher improve the students' flexibility in new situations? |

| WORKABLE OPTIONS: |

1. Praise students frequently when they make the slightest improvement toward change (e.g., "Bob, I see you're beginning your assignment. Keep up the good work!").

2. Reinforce students with a familiar and enjoyable special activity when they make adjustments in their understanding of a new concept, rule, and/or attitude.

3. Introduce new routines and/or instructional materials to the class via small groups or individually in order to minimize student anxiety.

4. Try to involve the students when making decisions about changes in classroom routines, so that they feel comfortable about the new procedures.

5. Explain change to any students who have been absent during the original introduction of the new process or procedure.

6. Use private conferences to make student aware of the need to be flexible.

7. Encourage students to slowly develop risk-taking skills so they may confront daily problems with new strategies.

8. Provide many opportunities for students to learn how to cope with their physical and social environment (e.g., role playing).

MANAGEMENT
PROBLEM: *POOR ATTITUDE IN AND TOWARD SCHOOL*

TEACHER'S
CONCERN: What can I do to improve a student's attitude in
                 school?

WORKABLE
OPTIONS: 1. Be enthused about the subject you are teaching
                 and sensitive to the needs of your students so the
                 students will develop favorable attitudes toward
                 the teacher and the subject.

                 2. Do not punish excessively or ridicule student
                 responses, or negative attitudes will develop toward
                 you and the subjects being taught. Sarcasm is a
                 negative and non-productive trait. Avoid it no
                 matter how frustrating a student may be to you.

                 3. Have a group discussion to promote insight into
                 the development of positive attitudes.

                 4. Use role playing to analyze productive and non-
                 productive attitudes.

                 5. Rather than reject a student's response completely,
                 find something positive to identify within this response
                 and move on from there. Rejection leads to
                 hopelessness and feeling of failure.

                 6. Give students the opportunity to experience
                 satisfaction with their attitudes so that they will be
                 reinforced.

                 7. Provide motivation in your classroom so children
                 will identify and be inspired in the formation of
                 sound values.

                 8. Provide a pleasant atmosphere in the classroom.
                 Make demands realistic and the curriculum more
                 suitable to meet the realistic needs of the students.

MANAGEMENT PROBLEM:	*POOR OR NON-EXISTENT WORK HABITS*

TEACHER'S CONCERN:	What do you do with students who do not complete their assigned work in class or at home?

WORKABLE
OPTIONS:

1. Have a class discussion on the importance of work in the community and being a responsible worker.

2. Have students set up career goals.

3. Relate success in school work to their success in their future vocations.

4. Keep a constant check on seatwork by moving around the classroom and glancing at students' progress.

5. Establish an agreement with the parents. Send home notes containing the student's work for that evening or call them during the day letting them know what the work is. If the work still is not done, obtain permission for after-school detention to complete the work.

6. Attach clear consequences to incomplete work (e.g., an additional assignment, being placed in another classroom to complete work, withholding a special project, etc.).

7. Institute a reward system to increase productivity. The reward must be meaningful - something the student wants (e.g., a homework excused pass, permission to use an interest center, etc.).

8. Confer with parents and help them establish a reward system for completing work and responsibilities around the house. Send home notes concerning completed work to be rewarded.

9. Mention the student to the school social worker. Perhaps there is something happening at home that prevents him/her from doing homework.

MANAGEMENT PROBLEM:	*PRIDE IN ONE'S WORK*
TEACHER'S CONCERN:	I would like to see the students take more pride in their work. What can I do?
WORKABLE OPTIONS:	1. Be sure that you, as an educator, set an example for the students to follow. Be a person who takes pride in his/her work (e.g., all work papers and letters sent home are neat and accurate, you are well prepared for each lesson, etc.).

2. Ask the students to evaluate their own work using the same grading system you use. This procedure will enable the children to reflect and decide upon the level and quality of their performance in school. Require that they give a rationale for their conclusions (e.g., why they deserve that grade).

3. Throughout the school year, have group discussions with the class about people in the past and present who have achieved significant accomplishments and made noteworthy contributions to society. Have them explore how these people demonstrated pride in their work.

4. Simply ask the student when submitting work if he/she is proud of his/her work. If they say no, take time to discuss the reason why. Grade papers for four aspects: complete, correct, concise, and comprehensive - the qualities basic to work well done.

5. Have one of the bulletin boards set aside for students to place any school work that they are proud to display for their parents to see at "Open House."

6. Show honest joy and enthusiasm for a well-done project or assignment.

MANAGEMENT PROBLEM:	*PUTTING PROPER IDENTIFICATION ON PAPERS*

TEACHER'S CONCERN:

How can children be taught to remember to put the correct identification on papers before turning them in?

WORKABLE OPTIONS:

1. Discuss with the class the importance of putting names on papers.

2. Remind children before actual work begins to place identification on papers.

3. Provide work clues such as: Name: _____ on worksheets.

4. Provide rewards for children who properly label work. Use stars, stickers, stamps, comments, etc.

5. Verbally praise children who correctly identify papers.

6. Attach an undesirable task as a consequence of forgetting to put names on work.

7. Make a personal reminder mobile. Use thick yarn and 3x5 cards. List in sequence the tasks needed to successfully complete a written task. Hang on each child's desk to be used as a guide.

8. Make a pride line using the student's name. List items that the child is proud of (e.g., Sue Jones - proud of her math score). This will help the child use his/her name for positive identification.

9. NEVER RIP UP OR DEFACE A PAPER BECAUSE THE NAME WAS FORGOTTEN. This is inappropriately severe punishment.

10. Choose a group captain for classroom chores. The captain checks to see if all have put their names on their papers before they are collected.

MANAGEMENT PROBLEM:	*QUIET ACTIVITIES FOR INDEPENDENT WORK*

TEACHER'S CONCERN: What are some suggestions for quiet activities for the children to do while waiting for others to finish work?

WORKABLE OPTIONS:

1. Students draw profiles and cut out pictures to paste on the profile that reflect their feelings/thoughts for that day or that represent their interests (e.g., skiing, hiking, reading, etc.).

2. Provide extra worksheets on areas of learning that have already been covered in class. Children love to do such work alone.

3. Provide books, videos, tape recorders, use of computer software, and puzzle materials for individual activities (interest corners).

4. Create an art box with extra art supplies. Children can create independent projects.

5. Provide projects such as hook rugs, pot holders, and ongoing creative materials.

6. Have a sheet of paper headed "I'm happiest when _____" and other incomplete sentences for students to complete.

7. Provide a worksheet with scrambled sentences and words.

8. Provide material for word searches.

9. Fill a reading bag with fun-to-read material such as classic comic books, greeting cards, riddles, etc..

10. Provide a class scrapbook for students to review.

11. Encourage the recording of information into daily diaries.

MANAGEMENT PROBLEM:	*RIVALRY TOWARD PEERS*

TEACHER'S CONCERN:

How can teachers help students improve in their cooperative behavior with peers?

WORKABLE OPTIONS:

1. Try to identify the factors within the classroom environment that may be contributing to the student's resentment of others (e.g., no friends, not enough positive attention, ridiculed by peers because of some idiosyncracy, etc.).

2. Talk to teachers who have taught the student in the past to obtain information about the student's sensitivity while working with his/her peers.

3. Give the student classroom responsibilities so that he/she may gain respect from the other students.

4. Encourage the student to talk to his/her classmates in a cooperative manner.

5. Converse with the student privately to help him/her see the kinds of problems he/she is creating with peers if that is the case.

6. Provide many occasions for the student to gain positive emotional support from his/her peers (e.g., group projects).

7. Get the student involved in peer tutoring so that he/she has first-hand experience with individual differences.

8. Use a peer rating procedure to determine the relative popularity position of each student in the class (sociogram).

MANAGEMENT PROBLEM:	*SHORT ATTENTION SPAN*
TEACHER'S CONCERN:	How do you manage students who have a very short attention span and find it very difficult to concentrate?
WORKABLE OPTIONS:	1. Check to see if the student has had a good breakfast and a good night's rest (Maslow's basic needs).

1. Check to see if the student has had a good breakfast and a good night's rest (Maslow's basic needs).

2. Use the services of school personnel to see if the student has any physical problems.

3. Make sure the lesson includes visual, auditory, and motor activities. Be sensitive to the student area of strength within the multiple intelligences (Howard Gardner).

4. Check to see that worksheets are neat, clear, and interesting to the students.

5. Use a cardboard carrel so that the student can better attend to what he/she is doing and not be distracted.

6. Avoid seating the student next to the window, the fish tank, the class pet, or near the door where hall activity can be observed.

7. Attention span may be increased if a motor activity is included, such as reading a story and then acting out the parts or making something to illustrate the story (hands-on activity).

8. For the lower grades, have short learning periods alternating with short activities so that the day is fast paced and varied.

MANAGEMENT PROBLEM:	*SILENT CHILD*
TEACHER'S CONCERN:	How do you relate to a silent child who does not react positively or negatively to compliments or complaints?
WORKABLE OPTIONS:	

1. If you consider the behavior serious, ask the Child Study Team to examine the situation.

2. Even if initially unsuccessful, continue to relate in a positive way to the child. This may eventually lead to a better relationship with the child.

3. Try to discover what interests the child has and then offer an opportunity to do some independent work in this area or partner this child with another who is more outgoing but sensitive.

4. Request a conference with the child's parent(s) and ask for their opinions or ideas.

5. Do a class sociogram and find out who the child would like to be with or considers a friend in the classroom. Seat them near each other. Perhaps a friendship will develop and the other child will be a good model.

6. Utilize the services of a counselor if such services are available in your school.

7. If the child is able and willing to accept it, give him/her a task that has a level of responsibility that would assure success (e.g., Ask the child to design and put up the next bulletin board and select other classmates to assist him/her. This project may open up the lines of communication between you and the student.).

MANAGEMENT PROBLEM:	*SITTING IN SEAT*

TEACHER'S CONCERN: What do you do with a student who is constantly out of his/her seat, putting feet in the aisle, and stretching across the chair rather than sitting in it?

WORKABLE OPTIONS:

1. Set clear rules as to self-control expected during academic periods.

2. Discuss safety rules and consequences of improper use of one's chair or putting one's feet in the aisle.

3. Place a student who has difficulty sitting still closer to your desk.

4. Reward whenever possible for correct behavior, even if it is only for a short period of time (e.g., send him/her on an errand, allow him/her to get a drink of water, etc.).

5. Be sure he/she has had a physical and has no health problems that make sitting still difficult (or impossible).

6. Try to ignore some behaviors and concentrate on students who are working well. This provides a model for the student who doesn't sit quietly and may encourage correct behavior.

7. Role play a classroom, with you being the student. Show examples of some of the habits the students exhibit and discuss them. Often very young students are not aware of this behavior and seeing it helps them understand the problem.

8. Provide adequate opportunity for movement around the classroom. Extended sitting in a desk is difficult for anyone, but may be nearly impossible for the very young.

MANAGEMENT PROBLEM:	*SOCIAL ADJUSTMENT OF NEW STUDENT*
TEACHER'S CONCERN:	What can be done to aid a new student in your class in his/her social adjustment?
WORKABLE OPTIONS:	1. Make a class sociogram. Determine the popular students and select one who will agree to be class host to new students to show them around the school.

1. Make a class sociogram. Determine the popular students and select one who will agree to be class host to new students to show them around the school.

2. Have the class share their answers to an open statement such as "The proudest time in my life was _____." Be sure the new student shares his/her answer with the class.

3. After getting to know a little about the new student, have each student write four positive observations about him/her. Read these aloud and let him/her keep them as a welcome to the class.

4. Have the students pair up, answer one or two questions given by you, and then switch partners. These questions should probe attitudes, which will allow the students to get to know one another.

5. Make available to the student or his/her parents the school handbook or catalog that provides the school's rules and regulations, floor plan with location of classes, information about the cafeteria, etc.

6. In the beginning, during recess, participate in the students' activities to see that the new student is included.

7. Be friendly and accepting of the new student. If the students have seen your acceptance, it may be easier for them to do the same.

8. Don't pressure the new student to adjust. Let him/her move at his/her own pace.

MANAGEMENT PROBLEM:	*STEALING*
TEACHER'S CONCERN:	What do you do when things are being taken from other students in the class? You ask the class to find it, and one student always finds what is missing. What do you do with students caught stealing?
WORKABLE OPTIONS:	

1. For the student who always finds what is missing, it might be prudent to quietly go to that student's desk after someone has reported something missing, and ask the student for it. Having him/her "find" it each time is giving him/her much attention and positive feedback for a negative action.

2. Discuss with the class the consequences of stealing in the outside world. A trip to the county jail, courthouse, or police station may be enlightening. A visit from a local policeman who will discuss the topic is also helpful.

3. Instruct the students to keep valuables in a safe place. Discourage them bringing valuables to school. Give them the option of giving you valuables (change from lunch money, etc.) for safekeeping until the end of the day.

4. Refer to a potentially stolen article as "lost" and ask students to "find" it.

5. Allow for privacy in returning "lost articles" so that you will have an opportunity to talk directly to the student.

6. Contact and inform parents if it is habitual behavior.

7. Explore the child's motive for stealing. Reasons such as poverty, attention, and desire need to be addressed, and alternate means of meeting these needs should be determined.

| MANAGEMENT PROBLEM: | *STEALING SCHOOL PROPERTY* |

| TEACHER'S CONCERN: | What kind of measures can be taken by teachers to discourage students from stealing school property? |

WORKABLE OPTIONS:

1. Provide classroom activities that expose students to the underlying principles of property rights of others (e.g., films, video, computer software, short stories, copyrights. etc. through class discussions, role playing, and research).

2. Try to determine the cause of stealing by privately talking to the student (e.g., uncontrollable urge, a lack of basic necessities, revenge upon others, forgetfulness, lack of a sense of responsibility, etc.).

3. Require that the student return the stolen object or reimburse the owner.

4. When students steal repeatedly, they should be severely reprimanded, the parents should be notified, and recommendations for counseling and review by the Child Study Team should be considered.

5. Students who cannot directly return the item or immediately reimburse the owner should be required to "work off" the amount and/or have the exact sum deducted from their weekly allowances or wages.

6. Emphasize the importance of a sense of trust among peers, the need for respect of other's possessions, and general discussions on alternative methods of obtain desired materials.

7. Make aware to the students through discussion or by publishing in the school policy handbook the consequences of taking school property. Follow up on the consequences consistently.

MANAGEMENT PROBLEM: *STORAGE SPACE FOR MINIMAL COST*

TEACHER'S CONCERN: What can be done to help increase storage space for students and teachers?

WORKABLE OPTIONS:

1. Obtain large cardboard boxes from stores. Decorate with attractive coverings. These may be stacked or lined up depending on what is stored inside.

2. Make a class building project. Use cinder blocks and boards to make bookshelves.

3. Purchase inexpensive metal shelving of various heights from hardware stores. Be sure they are firmly placed so that there is no chance of them falling over and injuring the teacher or children.

4. To store gym clothes and similar items. make duffel bags to be hung in the closet.

5. Enlist the help of the vocational-technical high school. Many times classes are eager to make projects such as shelves, closets, tables, etc.

6. Check your closets for out-of-date materials and tools you no longer use.

7. Catalog and organize all your materials so they are efficiently placed for strategic use.

MANAGEMENT PROBLEM:	*STRESS*

TEACHER'S CONCERN: How can I deal with the stress that I encounter as a classroom teacher?

WORKABLE OPTIONS:

1. Stress is not a problem, but rather a symptom. Focus on what is causing the stress. It may be classroom management, administrative pressure, lack of community support, home responsibilities, or lack of sleep, but the important decision is to take action. The appropriate action for each specific situation can be found in other sections of this publication.

2. If the stress is extreme, seek professional assistance.

3. It is possible that you have "maxed out" in your teaching skills and need a change. Investigate other professional areas in and out of education. Such a change can bring back the enthusiasm you once felt as a classroom teacher.

4. When experiencing a stressful situation, write down in a log the situation and how you are dealing with it. After a period of time, evaluate the log and see if a pattern develops. This information will assist you in making appropriate changes in your teaching.

5. When experiencing anxiety, share your feelings with the people with whom you are dealing. This may lower your level of stress after an incident.

6. Make a concerted effort to separate your stress-producing problems and handle one at a time. Once you have coped with one situation, that success often alleviates other situations that have led to a stessful reaction.

7. Evaluate your reactions and be sure you are not overreacting to the responsibilities placed upon you. You cannot solve everyone's problems!

MANAGEMENT PROBLEM:	*STUDENT ARGUES AND DENIES INVOLVEMENT IN A NEGATIVE ACTION*

TEACHER'S CONCERN:

A student is corrected for doing something wrong and becomes sarcastic. What do you do when he/she denies the action when he/she was clearly responsible?

WORKABLE OPTIONS:

1. Check to see if the discipline technique being used is too harsh or unfair.

2. Check to see if you are being consistent in your discipline for all students.

3. Do not confront the student in front of the group, which will put him/her on the defensive.

4. Don't make threats that cannot be carried out, such as "You will never go out to recess again." The student may lose respect for the teacher or not take the discipline seriously.

5. Clarify exactly what disruptive behavior the student has exhibited and exactly what the consequences will be.

6. Be firm in your voice tone, facial expressions, and gestures.

7. Highly praise a student who takes the consequences of disruptive behavior in a mature manner.

8. If a student is having a problem maintaining control, have a time out period for him/her to settle down before you continue to discuss concerns.

9. Role play arguments and discuss reactions.

10. Control your emotions so that you can rationally respond to the problem at hand.

MANAGEMENT PROBLEM:	*STUDENT CRITICISM*
TEACHER'S CONCERN:	What can I do when students constantly criticize each other?
WORKABLE OPTIONS:	

1. Have a classroom discussion concerning the students who are constantly criticizing each other. Be honest and show how it negatively affects the classroom atmosphere. Give the students an opportunity to share their feelings and concerns. Then give the students the responsibility of finding or developing solutions to this problem.

2. Through role play, share various techniques for expressing feelings without criticizing the person with whom you are communicating.

3. Many times the students who criticize or tease other students have low self-esteem. Therefore, try to create an atmosphere where everyone feels important, but not more important than anyone else in the class. This could be done by equally sharing the numerous responsibilities that lead to successful learning experiences in the classroom.

4. Try the following activity. Have the students sit in groups of five. Each student tells about himself/herself, and the other students list three positive attributes after listening to the student (thoughtful, sincere, artistic, talented, etc.). Each student shares these observations with the student who has just spoken. This demands that students find something positive about each other rather than something sarcastic and negative. It is often helpful to list positive words on the board (suggested by students) to help the students get into the "mood." This is especially effective with teenagers who find it difficult to express positive comments about each other.

MANAGEMENT PROBLEM:	*STUDENT HAS PERSONAL PROBLEM THAT SEEMS TO INTERFERE WITH HIS/HER PROGRESS, BUT HE/SHE HAS NOT SHARED THIS INFORMATION WITH THE TEACHER*
TEACHER'S CONCERN:	How can I help this student with his/her problem if he/she has not shared the problem with me?

WORKABLE OPTIONS:

1. Seek out the help of the guidance counselor and see if he/she has some information that can help you.

2. Check with the members of the Child Study Team and see if they can help you understand some of the student's concerns without infringing on the confidentiality to which the student is entitled.

3. Have a conference with the student to see if he/she can talk about what you feel is interfering with his/her academic progress.

4. Have a conference with the parents expressing your concern about the student and offering your support and assistance.

5. Encourage discussion of concerns and problems through formal and informal group sessions.

6. Do not pressure the student to reveal personal concerns that he/she does not wish to reveal. Work on building a rapport of trust and confidence with the student. When he/she is ready, he/she will share the problem with you.

MANAGEMENT	
PROBLEM:	*STUDENT WHO WORKS ACCURATELY BUT MORE RAPIDLY THAN OTHERS*
TEACHER'S	
CONCERN:	How does one cope with children who complete all work given to them in a minimal amount of time?

WORKABLE
OPTIONS:

1. Evaluate appropriateness of assignments. Determine whether such a child needs more challenging work.

2. Use an art box consisting of old art and material scraps. Such items fascinate children and help keep them busy. Make this box accessible to children upon completion of work.

3. Use learning centers such as "Things I Want to Know." Children supply questions and answers to each other's queries.

4. Establish a game area. Provide crossword puzzles on poster boards, jigsaw puzzles, pot holder making, hook rugs, etc. Provide activities that can be left and resumed easily at another time.

5. Provide a personal evaluation sheet. Such a sheet includes individual goals that the teacher would like the child to achieve. The child grades himself/herself after completion of each task. The teacher reviews this sheet at the end of each week and the child is rewarded for progress and independent work.

6. Provide a folder in some area of the room containing extra worksheets from assignments already completed. Let students select ones they like and work independently.

7. Allow these students to work on an independent project which involves the use of the library. When work is completed, students can request a library pass so that they may go to the library and do research on their project.

| MANAGEMENT PROBLEM: | *STUDENT WHO WORKS INACCURATELY AND RUSHES THROUGH ASSIGNMENTS* |

MANAGEMENT PROBLEM: *STUDENT WHO WORKS INACCURATELY AND RUSHES THROUGH ASSIGNMENTS*

TEACHER'S CONCERN: How can the tendency to work too quickly, but not accurately, be controlled?

WORKABLE OPTIONS:

1. Assign small quantities of work. Large amounts tend to make the children try to rush in order to accomplish all he/she is given to do.

2. Establish expected time limits for activities that are realistic. This will take the pressure off the child.

3. Do sample lessons with the children to help them learn to pace themselves while working.

4. Use bar graphs to indicate the length of time taken to complete an activity. Emphasize that the one who finishes first is not the winner in this game. It is the one who finishes correctly!

5. Discuss the consequences of working too quickly.

6. Attach an undesirable task to the end of an assignment if completed carelessly (e.g., rewriting).

7. Reward work prepared carefully with stickers or seals.

8. Do some work with the class to show the difference between quality and quantity of work. Relate this to shopping in the store (e.g., Would you like to buy five rotten oranges for 10 cents, or one large good one for 10 cents?).

9. Establish time schedules with the class that are reasonable.

*STUDENTS RUSHING TO LEAVE ROOM WHEN
BELL RINGS*

**TEACHER'S
CONCERN:**

What I dislike the most is when students pack up
their bookbags before class is even over in
anticipation of the end-of-period bell. What can I do
to stop that?

**WORKABLE
OPTIONS:**

1. Simply make it a class rule that students are not
permitted to pack up their bookbags until you say
it is time to do so. Also explain and discuss your
reasoning for this rule.

2. When the students do this consistently, it may
mean that they do not value the last five or ten
minutes of the class. You may want to evaluate
your lesson planning and make the end of your
teaching period more meaningful to the students.

3. On some of your tests, allow the students to use their
notes. Then the students will be aware of the value
of good note taking that represents the entire class
period.

4. Inform the students that a part of the grade for
the course will reflect how well the classroom time
is utilized.

5. It is not unusual for freshmen to be apprehensive
about the time allotted in moving from one class to
another. Assure these students that you will dismiss
them in time to get to their next class. Often these
students carry every book they need for the day in
their backpack because they are afraid that if they stop
at their locker they will not be on time for their next
class. It is important that you take this into
consideration and not have them worried that you will
extend the period and make them late for their next
class!

6. Practice your timing so that your lesson is not
rushed at the end of the period.

MANAGEMENT PROBLEM:	*SUBSTITUTE TEACHERS*
TEACHER'S CONCERN:	How can one be assured that the substitute reads and follows the plans you have left for him/her?
WORKABLE OPTIONS:	

1. Work out an arrangement with the main office so that the substitute will be given your plans immediately upon entering the building.

2. With your lesson plans, include a cover sheet. On the cover sheet print: "Please read lesson plans in entirety." Also include an evaluation sheet that permits the substitute to check off the areas covered with spaces for remarks on how well the students performed in each area, certain students who may need extra help, and suggestions.

3. Include your schedule and material list.

4. Prior to your absence, arrange with a neighboring teacher, familiar with your schedule, to look in on your class.

5. Appoint student helpers. List their names for the substitute as well as the duties for which they are responsible (e.g., give out or collect papers, line leader, etc.).

6. Maintain an organized classroom. Keep all teaching materials accessible to the substitute.

7. Establish a daily routine. Adhere to it. Such familiarity with a schedule will help the children be more comfortable with a substitute who follows the established schedule.

8. Establish a set of behaviors you feel constitutes proper management, and reinforce these expectations with the students. Students will understand that these rules are important in order to build a productive learning environment.

MANAGEMENT PROBLEM:	*TALKING IN THE CLASSROOM*

TEACHER'S CONCERN:

What do you do with students who continuously talk when they should be listening or working?

WORKABLE OPTIONS:

1. Give a warning or warning signal (e.g., flick of lights on and off). Then if talking persists, withhold a reward or give a punishment.

2. Reward or punish the entire class on occasion. (Peer pressure is a powerful force)

3. Try a strict behavior modification program. (See *Ticket Program* in Section II of this booklet.)

4. Discuss the importance of not talking and why talking is not allowed.

5. Establish times when talking is not allowed in the beginning of the school year.

6. Allow students free time to chat. This may cut down the talking out of turn.

7. During seatwork time, allow students to communicate through writing notes or whispering. Abuse of this privilege will result in some predetermined consequence.

8. Attach a consequence to the undesirable action. Keep an accurate record, preferably in the back of the pupil's record book, of when the infraction occurred so you can see if it follows a significant pattern (e.g., certain times of day, after certain activities, etc.) and plan changes to respond to this.

9. Confer with parents and help them establish a reward system for good days.

10. Separate talkers so the temptation is reduced.

11. Have lessons on manners, respect, etc.

MANAGEMENT PROBLEM:	*TANTRUMS*

TEACHER'S CONCERN:

How do I deal with a child who is throwing a tantrum (i.e., pushing his desk or books, screaming, crying, throwing objects, etc.)?

WORKABLE OPTIONS :

1. For safety's sake, remove him/her or have him/her removed from the classroom for the protection of other children.

2. Refer the student to the school disciplinarian as there may be a board policy for handling this.

3. Refer the child to the Child Study Team if this behavior is frequent; the child may need special placement.

4. Discuss proper behavior in the classroom and why it is expected in the beginning of the school year.

5. Students can brainstorm to provide alternative behaviors that are acceptable in dealing with disappointments, anger, frustration, etc.

6. Check into what caused the tantrum and try to structure the environment so that a tantrum is not triggered again.

7. Attach a consequence. Make sure the frequency (severity) of the offense is in direct proportion to the severity of the consequence. Keep an accurate record of when and why the tantrum happened and all other details.

8. Contact the parents. Try to obtain feedback on how they feel about this and if they have any idea what causes this behavior.

9. Attend seminars/workshops dealing with management skills. (Great film: "How Difficult Can It Be?" PBS Video, Alexandria, VA)

MANAGEMENT PROBLEM:	*TARDINESS*

TEACHER'S CONCERN:

What alternative strategies can teachers implement in their classrooms when a student's frequent tardiness disrupts the class?

WORKABLE OPTIONS:

1. Talk to the student privately to see if there is a valid reason for his/her tardiness.

2. Explain to students what measures will be taken if repeated violations occur.

3. Praise the students for their promptness (e.g., "It's nice to see that everyone arrived to class before the bell!").

4. Reward students for their promptness by allowing them to participate in a special weekly activity (e.g., listening to tapes, playing games, etc.).

5. Use group contingencies when several or more students are arriving late for class (e.g., "If all students enter the room before the bell rings, then the class will be able to watch a video during quiet time.").

6. Take from a student's free time the amount of time he/she is late for class (e.g., five minutes late means that the student stays five minutes extra).

7. Students who are excessively late (more than ten or fifteen minutes) and/or continually late for no apparent reason should be required to double the time that they must make up for their lateness.

8. Contact parents about the student's tardiness.

9. Inform principal or school counselor about students who are chronically late for a follow-up.

MANAGEMENT PROBLEM:	*TELEVISION AND THE INTERNET*

TEACHER'S CONCERN:

It seems to me that the students watch too much television and spend too much time "surfing the net." Is there anything I can do about this?

WORKABLE OPTIONS:

1. Have a meeting with the parents to ask for their opinions and suggestions for solving this problem.

2. Although it is a value judgement, assist the students in selecting some of the shows they watch on TV and the amount of time they spend "surfing the net." This may improve the quality of the programs they watch and a more thoughtful selection of Internet materials.

3. Discuss with the students other types of activities they could experience and enjoy other than these sedentary ones.

4. Ask the students to record the number of hours they watch television or spend with their computer each week. Also have them list what else they do during that week. Have cooperative learning groups develop an evaluative scale that will be able to measure the quality use of their time.

5. Introduce the students to other community activities and services available to them. Bring in speakers to present these options.

6. Have books available in the classroom that represent areas of the students' interest. Have weekly book reviews where students will discuss the concepts of stories they have read. Initiate a paperback book exchange.

7. Have students choose a program and write an evaluative review using a general questionnaire that asks: "What have you learned? How was the quality of acting (was it realistic and believable)? Did it discuss a positive or negative aspect of life?"

MANAGEMENT PROBLEM:	*TRUANCY*

TEACHER'S CONCERN:

How can teachers improve their students' attitudes toward school when the reasons for their poor attendance are boredom, non-caring attitude, and peer pressure?

WORKABLE OPTIONS:

1. Plan class trips through the community and/or to public buildings, parks, and historical sites to make school as interesting as possible for the students.

2. Try to motivate the student to get involved in constructive athletics or club activities where others depend upon his/her being present.

3. Make adjustments in the student's program whenever possible (e.g., late arrival, early dismissal, half day schedule, etc.) if requested by the Child Study Team or counselor. Be flexible. Let the student know how pleased you are to have him/her in your class. BE SINCERE!

4. Begin a reward system to reinforce when the student comes to school (e.g., "Each day you are in school, you will receive a credit toward a special weekly activity of your own choosing.").

5. Provide individual counseling for the student to try to discover why he/she avoids school.

6. Send a registered letter to the parents noting weekly school absences (after you have tried to contact them by telephone and if it is school policy) noting the legal consequences of truancy.

7. Contact the school attendance officer for a home visit if the problem becomes severe.

8. Give a monthly report to the administration and/or supervisors about students who have an excessive number of absences (e.g., ten or more days absent in a given time period).

SECTION II

A CLASSROOM MANAGEMENT SYSTEM

A TICKET TO CLASSROOM MANAGEMENT SUCCESS
Designed by :   Ann Weinbrenner

I. INTRODUCTION

This is a recipe for positive reinforcement based on a ticket system which rewards
acceptable behavior and penalizes unacceptable behavior. This allows the students
to clearly identify right from wrong. Within this program there is always the
opportunity for a student to correct a wrongdoing and change unacceptable
behavior into acceptable behavior.

II. OBJECTIVES

With the implementation of this program the students will be able to:

- identify and respond to basic classroom rules

- establish parameters clarifying these rules to help prevent them from
stepping "over the line" and getting penalized for breaking
rules of which they were unaware

- demonstrate an awareness of self-worth, self-respect, and self-
discipline

- demonstrate an understanding of the outcome of both positive and
negative behavior

- demonstrate sensitivity and awareness of the need to respect others

III. BASIC COMPONENTS

In order to implement this program, it is necessary to understand the basic
components that allow the teacher to demonstrate clearly to the students whether
or not they have successfully fulfilled the requirements of behavior so important in
building a productive learning environment. The procedure for getting started is as
follows:

On the first day of school (or whenever introducing the system), post on the
blackboard or on a bulletin board the following clarifying information:

GREEN TICKET - POSITIVE BEHAVIOR
GOLD TICKET- VALUE OF 10 GREEN TICKETS
SILVER TICKET - ISSUED FOR EARNING 10 GOLD TICKETS

Upon receipt of the SILVER TICKET, the student is recognized as student of the month in the classroom.

Other tickets in the system are:

RED TICKET - UNACCEPTABLE BEHAVIOR
BLACK TICKET - ISSUED AFTER 5 RED TICKETS

The BLACK TICKET leads to detention.

In addition to the above ticket system described, there is need for supportive rewards for the students, which is provided as follows:

l. Reward Box with things in it which student may reach in and "grab" after receipt of a GOLD TICKET.

2. ICE CREAM TICKET when the SILVER TICKET is achieved (often cost is provided by PTA).

3. A mystery gift when a second SILVER TICKET is received (donated by local merchants).

4. A chance surprise when withdrawing color tickets from ticket box.

IV. PROCESS

All behavior is judged on concrete and tangible activities of the students. This includes class conduct and homework. The student's effort is the primary indicator of his/her success or failure to receive tickets. There is no misunderstanding regarding right and wrong for this is clearly defined throughout the day in all activities.

At the beginning of each day, the student rates him/herself, when the teacher calls the roll, in regard to his/her conduct of the previous day. When a student's name is called he replies "YES" if his/her conduct was acceptable and "NO" if his/her conduct was unacceptable.

The same procedure applies to homework with the students responding "COMPLETE" or "INCOMPLETE".

On the front of each student's desk is a plastic holder into which the earned tickets are placed each day. These tickets are displayed for everyone to see.

If a student answers "YES" and "COMPLETE" all week, he/she has received a green ticket for each day. On Friday his/her name goes up on the HONORS BULLETIN BOARD.

The student achieving a YES and COMPLETE for an entire month receives a monthly certificate signed and issued by the principal.

V. MATERIALS

Tickets are 2" x 2" squares cut from the appropriate color construction paper and kept in a shoe box marked with the respective colors (green, gold, red, or black). As each student earns a ticket, as an added incentive, he/she picks from the appropriate box without looking. If the student picks a green ticket with a smiling face stamped on it, the student is then eligible to pick a "grabber" which has different fun things in them, such as to be first in line, skip an assignment, etc.

If the class receives a compliment from anyone other than the classroom teacher (specials, principal, visitor) they get two green tickets. They also can lose a green ticket if they do something unacceptable, but they may earn it back by improved behavior. If anyone gets a red ticket he/she can work it off by doing what they did wrong correctly, such as not calling out in class or annoying another student.

CERTIFICATES AWARDED CAN BE EASILY DESIGNED WITH ANY PRINT COMPUTER SOFTWARE.

VI: SUMMARY BY CREATOR OF SYSTEM

"I have used this system for over 13 years and it works better every year. Once it gets started it is so motivating that within weeks, red tickets are no longer needed. Everyone's day is usually pleasant and happy and the students become very aware and sensitive to the needs of others."

A Way of Life
Know how to have respect for myself and others...
Involve myself as an active and good citizen...
Never lie or hurt others...
Do to others what you want them to do to you...

Discipline is a mode of learning that demonstrates positive and moral behavior. Discipline reflects the three basic concepts:
1. love your students
2. trust your students
3. be gentle but firm in your classroom management

It takes love, consistency and record keeping everyday, but the rewards for the teacher and students are so fulfilling it is worth the extra effort."

Ann Weinbrenner

Discipline is a mode of learning that demonstrates positive and moral behavior. Discipline reflects the three basic concepts:

1. love your students

2. trust your students

3. be gentle but firm in your class-room management.

ADDITIONAL RESOURCES

Burden, Paul R. Classroom Management and Discipline: Methods to Facilitate
    Cooperation and Instruction. New York: Longman, 1995.

Dubelle, Stanley T. Student Self Discipline: Helping Students Behave
    Responsibly. Rockport, ME: ProActive Publications, 1995.

Gordon, Ann. Guiding Young Children in a Diverse Society. Boston: Allyn &
    Bacon, 1996.

Harmin, Merrill. Inspiring Discipline: A Practical Guide for Today's Classrooms
    West Haven, CT: NEA Professional Library, 1995.

Kohn, Alfie. Beyond Discipline: From Compliance to Community. Alexandria,
    VA: ASCD, 1996.

Perro, Ann. Talk it Out: Conflict Resolution in the Elementary Classroom.
    Alexandria, VA: ASCD, 1996.

Ross, Dorothea M. Childhood Bullying and Teasing: What School Personnel,
    Other Professionals, and Parents Can Do. Alexandria, VA: American
    Counseling Association, 1996.

Wielkiewicz, Richard M. Behavior Management in the Schools: Principles and
    Procedures. Second Edition. Boston: Allyn & Bacon, 1995.

Wolfgang, Charles H. Solving Discipline Problems: Methods & Models for
    Today's Teachers. Third Edition. Boston: Allyn & Bacon, 1995.

114